Acce
Genera

Eur
Des

Walt

LEARNING
RESOURCE
CENTRE

TRC
THOMAS ROTHERHAM COLLEGE
A tradition of achievement - A future of opportunity

D1513515

Hodder & Stoughton
LONDON SYDNEY AUCKLAND

The cover illustration shows a portrait of Catherine the Great (courtesy Michael Holford)

Other titles in the series:

Spain: Rise and Decline 1474–1643
Jill Kilsby   ISBN 0 340 51807 3

From Revolt to Independence: The Netherlands 1550–1650
Martyn Rady   ISBN 0 340 51803 0

Russia, Poland and the Ottoman Empire 1725–1800
Andrina Stiles   ISBN 0 340 53334 X

France in Revolution
Duncan Townson   ISBN 0 340 53494 X

The Unification of Italy 1815–70
Andrina Stiles   ISBN 0 340 51809 X

The Unification of Germany 1815–90
Andrina Stiles   ISBN 0 340 51810 3

British Library Cataloguing in Publication Data
Oppenheim, Walter
    Europe and the enlightened despots.—(Access to history).
    1. Europe. Absolutism, history
    I. Title   II. Series
    321.6094

ISBN 0 340 53559 8

First published 1990
Second impression 1992

Typeset by Wearside Tradespools, Fulwell, Sunderland
Printed in Great Britain for the educational publishing
division of Hodder and Stoughton Ltd, Mill Road, Dunton
Green, Sevenoaks, Kent by Page Bros Ltd, Norwich.

Contents

Preface

To the general reader

Although the *Access to History* series has been designed with the needs of students studying the subject at higher examination levels very much in mind, it also has a great deal to offer the general reader. The main body of the text (i.e. ignoring the Study Guides at the ends of chapters) forms a readable and yet stimulating survey of a coherent topic as studied by historians. However, each author's aim has not merely been to provide a clear explanation of what happened in the past (to interest and inform): it has also been assumed that most readers wish to be stimulated into thinking further about the topic and to form opinions of their own about the significance of the events that are described and discussed (to be challenged). Thus, although no prior knowledge of the topic is expected on the reader's part, she or he is treated as an intelligent and thinking person throughout. The author tends to share ideas and possibilities with the reader, rather than passing on numbers of so-called 'historical truths'.

To the student reader

There are many ways in which the series can be used by students studying History at a higher level. It will, therefore, be worthwhile thinking about your own study strategy before you start your work on this book. Obviously, your strategy will vary depending on the aim you have in mind, and the time for study that is available to you.

If, for example, you want to acquire a general overview of the topic in the shortest possible time, the following approach will probably be the most effective:

1　Read Chapter 1 and think about its contents.
2　Read the 'Making notes' section at the end of Chapter 2 and decide whether it is necessary for you to read this chapter.
3　If it is, read the chapter, stopping at each heading or * to note down the main points that have been made.
4　Repeat stage 2 (and stage 3 where appropriate) for all the other chapters.

If, however, your aim is to gain a thorough grasp of the topic, taking however much time is necessary to do so, you may benefit from carrying out the same procedure with each chapter, as follows:

1　Read the chapter as fast as you can, and preferably at one sitting.
2　Study the flow diagram at the end of the chapter, ensuring that you understand the general 'shape' of what you have just read.

3   Read the 'Making notes' section (and the 'Answering essay questions' section, if there is one) and decide what further work you need to do on the chapter. In particularly important sections of the book, this will involve reading the chapter a second time and stopping at each heading and * to think about (and to write a summary of) what you have just read.
4   Attempt the 'Source-based questions' section. It will sometimes be sufficient to think through your answers, but additional understanding will often be gained by forcing yourself to write them down.

When you have finished the main chapters of the book, study the 'Further Reading' section and decide what additional reading (if any) you will do on the topic.

This book has been designed to help make your studies both enjoyable and successful. If you can think of ways in which this could have been done more effectively, please write to tell me. In the meantime, I hope that you will gain greatly from your study of History.

Keith Randell

CHAPTER 1

Introduction: Enlightened Despotism

1 The *Ancien Régime*

One of the myths about the French Revolution of 1789 is that it destroyed a static and backward-looking society, first in France and then in the rest of Europe. Soon after the Revolution began, people started to use the phrase *ancien régime* to describe the old system of government in France before 1789. The phrase has since grown in meaning to encompass the social system as well as the systems of government in most eighteenth-century European states. The phrase conjures up an image of kings and queens who lived in luxurious palaces like Versailles, wielding absolute power without any form of representative assembly to limit them, whilst the peasants, often serfs in eastern Europe, paid their excessive taxes, scratched a living from their small fields and starved. The nobility are seen as parasites, doing no work and living off the hard labour of the peasants. The nobles, who had long since ceased to perform any useful function in society, now gathered round the royal family to entertain and be entertained. Fortunately, however, the French Revolution then took place, sweeping away a corrupt and inefficient society and replacing it with the modern nation-state – a state based on representative government where promotion was on merit and privilege was abolished.

As with many other myths, not all these oversimplifications are totally without foundation. It is, however, misleading to see eighteenth-century governments as being static and backward-looking. On the contrary, the years before 1789 saw many of the monarchs adopting radically new approaches towards their subjects. These monarchs, of whom the best known are Frederick II of Prussia (1740–86), Catherine II of Russia (1762–96) and Joseph II of Austria (1780–90) are called the Enlightened Despots, although this was not a term that they used themselves. These monarchs saw their role not as one where they had been put on earth to enjoy themselves at the expense of the peasants, but one where they were given responsibility for developing the state and for providing protection and some element of welfare for all their people. They rejected the luxurious lifestyle of a previous generation of monarchs and concentrated on the work of modernising their states. They saw themselves as the servants, rather than the masters, of their states.

Their efforts were not always consistent or successful, and their attitudes towards the privileges of the nobility were often equivocal, but these monarchs were nevertheless moving far closer towards creating the modern state than the phrase *ancien régime* and the image of Versailles suggest. It is in fact possible to argue, as Simon Schama does in *Citizens*, his history of the French Revolution, that in many ways the Revolution hindered this progress towards the modern state which had been started by the monarchs of Europe. During the seventeenth century most monarchs had seen no reason to justify their existence to their subjects. The existence of monarchy was closely linked with religion, and therefore not open to question by most people. The coronation ceremony emphasised the ties with the Church and stressed the semi-divine nature of monarchy. Bossuet, the confessor to Louis XIV of France (1643–1715), put forward the doctrine known as the Divine Right of Kings, using scripture to argue that God placed kings on earth. Kings were answerable only to God, and only He could punish them if they broke the Commandments. People had to obey their kings without question; to disobey or even to question a monarch was as serious a matter as disobeying God.

Other writers who turned their attention to political theory came to similar conclusions to Bossuet. Both Jean Bodin in France and Thomas Hobbes in England were deeply influenced by the civil wars which had taken place in their countries during their lifetimes. They both wrote books advocating absolute monarchy, not on religious grounds as Bossuet had done, but because the alternative to a strong monarchy was chaos and destruction. At this time the only alternatives to a strong monarch were civil war, or rule by the nobility. The state where the nobles most obviously controlled the government was Poland. The chaotic state of this country, which was eventually to lead to its destruction, was not a good advertisement for alternatives to absolutism.

Absolute monarchy was an appropriate system of government during a period of history when religion was the strongest influence over people's behaviour and beliefs, and where the only alternatives were worse. However, no king had actually reached the total power advocated by Bossuet and Hobbes. Even in France, at that time regarded as the pinnacle of absolutism, Louis XIV might proclaim proudly that '*L'État c'est moi*', but in reality he had to share his power with other individuals and groups, including the nobles, the Church and the *parlements* (courts). Louis XIV, who professed absolutism, was never able or willing to totally suppress them. Instead he and his royal officials had to work alongside them. Even Louis XIV was answerable, not just to God, but to the traditions and customs of his state, and these he was careful to respect.

During the eighteenth century the Divine Right of Kings, already more a theory justifying absolutism than a reflection of what really happened, became increasingly discredited. Whilst the coronation ceremony was retained everywhere, other practices which symbolised the monarch's divine status fell into disuse. These included the practice of kings claiming to cure disease by touching the afflicted person. Very few kings now believed, and none asserted, that they had been placed on earth by God to rule absolutely. Instead monarchs looked for other ways to justify their power and existence and it was this that led to the idea that royal power was necessary to protect the state and its people. This was not, as Lord Acton, the famous nineteenth-century historian claimed, because the monarchs were on the defensive. None ever felt the need to apologise for the power they enjoyed. On the contrary, they were anxious to increase their powers further, and could give good reasons for doing so.

* The decline of Divine Right monarchy came at the same time as Europe began to change in other ways, and there is no doubt that the shift to Enlightened Despotism reflected these changes. The four main changes were: The influence of the great explorations; the effects of the religious wars of the sixteenth and seventeenth centuries; the Scientific Revolution of the seventeenth century; and the impact of the 'Glorious Revolution' in England in 1688. As a result of these influences an increasing number of writers, most of them French, came to question Divine Right monarchy and – sometimes – to offer alternatives. These writers are collectively known as the *philosophes*, although their writings were often more narrow in range than the English translation 'philosophers' would suggest. Monarchs who had read these books, or at least knew of their ideas, and then attempted to put some of them into practice, were the ones subsequently given the accolade of 'Enlightened Despot'. Later chapters will look at what reforms these monarchs did introduce, and to what extent they owed their basis to the writings of the *philosophes*; but first it will be necessary to look at the influences that produced the *philosophes*.

2 Changing Europe

Political change never takes place in isolation. Eighteenth-century rulers were as vulnerable as those of today to new social and economic forces. It was largely developments in areas outside politics which suggested to both writers and monarchs that changes to the systems of government were desirable.

a) The Great Explorations

The great explorations, which had started in the fifteenth century with Portuguese and Spanish ships seeking a direct route to the spice islands of the East, were to have a major impact on the ways in which European people thought about themselves. By the eighteenth century much of the world had been discovered, colonies were being established abroad, and an increasing range of food, clothing and precious metals from other continents was reaching the upper classes in Europe. The

See Preface for explanation of * symbol.

explorations made educated people aware of the vast range of religions and systems of government that existed elsewhere. The considerable interest that stories about these faraway places aroused is indicated by the success of such books as *The Arabian Nights* and *Sinbad the Sailor*, which were published in Europe for the first time during the eighteenth century.

Europeans made the disturbing discovery that religions existed which were much older than Christianity and which preached similar moral values. Societies came to light which existed in America and Africa without formal governments or laws, but where the people lived in harmony with each other with high moral standards and no crime. Europeans had previously believed that absence of strong government always led to barbarism and war, but this was now called into question. The explorations also raised the uncomfortable question as to whether Christianity was essential for civilisation to exist. In time the concept of the 'Noble Savage' – the primitive man who lived peacefully, morally and happily – became popular. Here was an alternative way of life and government which, whilst impractical in European terms, did call into question the easy assumptions of an earlier generation of political theorists that the only alternative to absolutism was chaos.

b) Religious Wars

The old unity and strength of the Church had been broken in the sixteenth century by the Reformation. Not only was Christianity now split between Roman Catholicism and Protestantism, but a series of damaging religious wars weakened the authority of the Church even further. Eventually monarchs were able to assert their right to choose the religion for their state. Instead of the monarch being reliant on the support of the Church to justify his position, the Church was now dependent on the monarchy for its continued existence as the official church of the country. Monarchs in countries as diverse as Russia and France were able to assert the primacy of the state over the Church. State control over church lands and clerical appointments was usual in most of Europe before 1700. At the same time the impact of printing threatened the Church's monopoly over what was read and what was taught in school and university. Churches – particularly the Roman Catholic Church – continued to assert that they held a monopoly of truth and wisdom and that they had the right to decide what people could be allowed to read, but this was becoming increasingly difficult to achieve in practice. The Reformation and the spread of the printing press had combined to create the modern secular state, and one in which the theory of Divine Right was becoming an anachronism.

c) The Scientific Revolution

Significant developments were made in science during the seventeenth century. The scientific method of hypothesis tested by experiment was established. Mathematics advanced with the invention of logarithms and calculus and the development of algebra. New instruments – the telescope and microscope – enabled scientists to look both outwards to the universe and inwards to the mysteries of the human body. The results were startling. Not only were previously unknown forms of life discovered by the microscope, but the work of the astonomers Copernicus and Galileo demonstrated that the sun, not the earth, was the centre of the known universe. This was disturbing for the Church, which had argued that God had placed the earth at the centre of the universe. The Inquisition forced Galileo to retract his statements when he pressed them too strongly, but this did not solve the problem, since the Church's view could only be justified by faith, whilst the astronomers could demonstrate what they claimed. Men like Galileo had no wish to attack or undermine the Church; they thought of themselves as good Christians who were only seeking to understand the mysteries and wonders of God's universe. In reality, their findings and the Catholic Church's reaction to them seriously undermined the credibility of the Church. Not only were men now seeking to find out for themselves, rather than taking the Church's word for what went on in the universe, but their findings suggested that perhaps the Church was not always right in its interpretation.

Towering over the other scientists in the seventeenth century was the figure of Sir Isaac Newton (1642–1727). In his *Principia Mathematica* he set out his Laws on Motion. However, his book was far more than an explanation of how gravity works. By offering a mathematical explanation of why planets revolved round the sun in their eliptical paths, he also suggested that the whole material and scientific world could be explained by fundamental Laws of Nature. The universe, despite its complexity and apparent random nature, could now be explained by science. Furthermore these Laws were capable of being understood, and those which were not yet known were waiting to be discovered. This task, which scientists have enthusiastically taken up ever since, meant that Newton offered the hope that one day every aspect of the universe could be understood through scientific laws.

The eighteenth century saw the creation and development of several new sciences as men tried to find out and record why things happened. Amongst these were Botany, Biology and Geology. Most of the scientists, including Newton himself, were believers in God who were trying to understand how His universe worked. Yet they repeatedly found that their discoveries contradicted the Church's teachings, and so raised further doubts in the minds of educated people about whether the Church really did hold a monopoly of the truth.

Newton's greatest significance was his contention that the universe could be explained and understood through knowledge of scientific laws. He even suggested that such laws might also apply to the fields of human behaviour, and so encouraged others to look for these laws. All aspects of human life were placed under the scrutiny of writers and, in the process, the eighteenth century saw the invention of Economics, Sociology and Anthropology. Government and the role of monarchy was also studied, and existing ideas called into question. Europe entered an age when Reason and the search for scientific laws would replace faith and tradition amongst the educated minority.

It is doubtful whether any of these explorations into political theory would have had as much impact as they did without the existence of a country which had proved that there was a workable alternative to absolute monarchy. The practical success of the English Revolution of 1688 was at least as important as the Scientific Revolution in bringing into question previous assumptions about the nature of government.

d) The English Revolution

In the 'Glorious Revolution' of 1688 King James II of England was overthrown because of opposition to his policies which, it was believed, were turning Britain into a Catholic absolute monarchy. He was replaced by William III who was obliged to accept his role as a limited monarch, with much of the real power held by a parliament whose lower house was made up of elected members. Far from bringing England to the point of collapse, this experiment in limited monarchy proved to be remarkably successful. During the eighteenth century British strength grew rapidly. Agricultural and industrial revolutions turned England into the most advanced and prosperous country in the world, whilst at the same time her colonial empire rapidly outstripped her rivals. Economic progress might have been ignored by European monarchs as being unconnected with the system of government, but there was no escaping the increased military strength of the British. From the Battle of Blenheim (1704) onwards, both the army and navy won a succession of battles culminating in the British triumph over France in the Seven Years War (1756–63). By this time Britain had emerged as one of the strongest states in Europe. One of the chief arguments of absolute monarchy had been that only such a system allowed the concentration of military resources needed to protect the state. Britain proved that it was possible to achieve political stability, economic strength and military power without absolute monarchy. The contrast between the Britain of 1670, with its absolute monarchy but insignificant role in Europe and undeveloped economy, and that of 1770, with a limited monarchy, but also a well developed economy and a military, naval and colonial power second to none, was not lost on

Europe in 1740

contemporaries. Many writers, including Voltaire and Montesquieu, admired Britain and recommended that other states should follow her example.

*   England had also produced a writer to give eloquent justification for limited monarchy – John Locke (1632–1704). In his *Letters on Toleration* he was the first to argue in favour of a limited degree of religious toleration. More important was his *Treatise on Civil Government*. In this book he put forward the idea of the Social Contract, which was to have immense influence on the French *philosophes*. He believed that governments had been established by men to give them life, property, security and maximum freedom. As long as a monarch provided these needs the people were obliged to obey him; but if the monarch ever abused his power, as James II had done, then he had broken the contract with his people. Under these circumstances the people had not just the right, but the *duty* to overthrow their monarch, who had now forfeited his throne, and replace him with one who would fulfil his obligations to his people – a William III, for example.

Locke justified what had already happened in England on theoretical grounds. He was not arguing for democracy; the rights of people, including the right to overthrow a monarch, were limited to people who already had wealth and status. However, despite these limitations, Locke's work broke new ground and argued for a totally new principle of government – that it was for the benefit of the people, and that the monarch was answerable for his actions. Many of the *philosophes* were deeply impressed, both with Locke's writings, and with the practical success of England compared with their own decaying absolute monarchy. This was reflected in the admiration for all things English which became fashionable in France during the eighteenth century – from afternoon tea to informal landscaped gardens. More importantly, it led a number of French writers to develop Locke's arguments further.

Making Notes on 'Introduction: Enlightened Despotism'

For this chapter you will only need to make brief notes. These should enable you to gain some idea of the nature of monarchy before the eighteenth century, the reasons why this system of monarchy became discredited in the eighteenth century, and an initial idea of what is meant by 'Enlightened Despotism'. Don't worry if at this stage you are tentative about what the term means. You will increase your understanding of this as you work your way through the rest of the book, and you will be able to provide a much more comprehensive definition when you have finished.

The following headings and questions may be helpful to you in making your notes. Remember that one sentence is all you will need to write under most headings.

1   The *ancien régime*
1.1. Explain what the term means
1.2. What were the justifications put forward for absolute monarchy in the seventeenth century?
1.3. The move to Enlightened Despotism
1.4. Explain what the term Enlightened Despotism means
2   Changing Europe
2.1. The significance of the Explorations
2.2. The declining importance of the Church and the invention of printing
2.3. The Scientific Revolution and the impact of Isaac Newton
2.4. The English Revolution
2.5. The ideas of John Locke

CHAPTER 2

The Writers of the Enlightenment

1 Montesquieu

Charles de Secondat, better known as the Baron de Montesquieu (1689–1755) was arguably the most influential of the *philosophes*, and the one whose theories have had the most impact on the systems of government used by states today. He was the son of a minor nobleman, but at the age of 27 inherited from his uncle the post of President of the *Parlement* of Bordeaux. He held the post for ten years and then sold it, but never ceased to be a defender both of the nobility in general, and of their privileged position in the French legal system in particular. After leaving his post he travelled widely in Europe, and was particularly influenced by his stay in England from 1729 to 1731, during which time he studied Locke's writings, frequently attended debates in Parliament, and studied the English system of government. He was, like other writers, impressed with the English system, which seemed to be far more successful than the outmoded and inefficient absolutism of his own monarch, Louis XV.

Montesquieu wrote many books on a wide variety of subjects, but his fame is largely based on just two of these – *Lettres Persanes* (Persian Letters) which was published in 1721 and his supreme achievement, *De l'Esprit des Lois* (Spirit of the Laws), which took him 20 years to write and which was published towards the end of his life in 1748.

* *Lettres Persanes* appeared at a time when there was great interest in the Orient. Two imaginary educated Persians are travelling round Europe and write home their thoughts on what they see. As outsiders they are able to comment critically and sarcastically on the faults they find in 'civilised' Europe. Montesquieu was therefore able to pour his own scorn on the people and institutions he despised, whilst protecting himself from the censor by claiming that these were, of course, only the views of some ignorant imaginary foreigners, not of the author himself. With wit, subtlety and style Montesquieu attacked the powerful, including Tax-Farmers, the Jesuits, doctors, the theatre, the French Academy, religious intolerance and persecution, the Inquisition and absolute monarchy itself. He included stinging attacks on the recently dead and officially revered Louis XIV of France. The *Lettres* established Montesquieu's reputation, but more importantly it broke new ground, in evading censorship and encouraging others to follow the author's lead in denouncing what they felt to be wrong in society.

* *De l'Esprit des Lois* is one of the most important books in the history of political theory, but it is hardly read today. There has not been, for example, an English translation of it for over 200 years. By modern standards it is an extremely badly organised and over-long book with its

595 chapters. The book was promptly placed on the *Index* by the Roman Catholic Church. This was the list of books which Catholics were forbidden to read, but despite (or because of) this attempt to stop the faithful reading it, the book was a best-seller in France.

The key chapters of the book put forward Montesquieu's views on government. He argued that there were three types of government. There was absolute monarchy as widely practised in Europe at the time. This was usually a bad system of government, although it might suit some countries if there were special circumstances. Unfortunately the lack of restraint imposed on the monarch all too often led to despotism and rule by fear. The second type was the Republic, based on 'The Will of the People'. This was an appropriate form of government for small states such as Venice or the Roman Republic of old. It worked only when power resided in the hands of an educated, unselfish and virtuous élite, but was unsuitable for most large states.

* Montesquieu argued that the best system for larger states was mixed monarchy. Here he relied heavily on the teachings of Locke and what he thought happened in England, although in fact he misunderstood the English system of government in some ways. In his mixed monarchy the king appointed ministers who were responsible for carrying out the laws. The king could also veto laws of which he disapproved, but he could not make his own laws. The legislature should be a two-house assembly as in England; a house for the nobility and an elected house based on a limited franchise. These two houses would jointly make the laws and vote the taxes. Finally, the judiciary would play a key role in enforcing the laws. Montesquieu's vigorous argument advocating an independent judiciary, free from any government interference and separate from the other two organs of government, reflected his experiences as President of the Bordeaux *Parlement*.

* The idea of the 'Separation of Powers' was a new one which developed Locke's theories into a practical model. At the time no state copied his ideas, but in the long run they were to have an immense influence. Catherine II was impressed with his arguments and incorporated many of them into her *Nakaz* of 1767 (see page 62), the French *parlements* in the 1760s and 1770s used Montesquieu to justify their opposition to Louis XV's attempts to undermine their power; similar arguments were used by the Hungarian and Belgian nobility when they resisted Joseph II of Austria in the 1780s. When the thirteen colonies broke away from Britain and became the United States of America in the 1770s, they turned to Montesquieu when writing their constitution, and to this day the system of government in the USA remains the most successful example of Montesquieu's ideas in practice. The French revolutionaries of 1789 had also read their Montesquieu, and the short-lived constitution of 1791 was partly based on his ideas. Montesquieu's attacks on absolute monarchy, his advocacy of the 'Separation of Powers', and his defence of the privileges and powers of the nobility as providing essential protection against despotism were attractive to a wide range of people.

However, *De l'Esprit des Lois* is a significant book for reasons other than its political message. Montesquieu's studies convinced him that different types of society are moulded by different factors, and that contrary to Newton's arguments, there was no single simple set of laws which determined the make up of a society. This was why he gave his book its title; he felt that there was a real 'Spirit' to laws, which would vary from state to state. Amongst the influences he identified were religion, climate, customs and history. He paid particular attention to climate, arguing, for instance, that it was Russia's cold climate that made the people respond only to force and which made despotism a suitable form of government for them. It is easy today to criticise the emphasis which Montesquieu placed on climate, but the important point is that it represented a breakthrough in the study of social, economic and historical factors in a state. Montesquieu had invented the study of Sociology.

Montesquieu also argued for a change to the criminal law so as to try to reform rather than punish criminals, thus anticipating Beccaria's much better-known book on crime. He criticised the establishment of colonies and argued that the state existed to protect the poor. He was one of the few *philosophes* to look critically at foreign policy, arguing that arms races increased tension and the likelihood of wars, and urging that they should stop before mankind invented a weapon that could kill everyone. He had produced a wide-ranging book which offered a new view of society and argued for a tolerant, benevolent monarchy with limited powers which avoided wars and governed in order to protect the people. It was one of the most influential books ever written, and one which was far more constructive than the more famous books which followed.

2 Diderot and the *Encyclopédie*

Denis Diderot (1713–84) came from relatively humble origins and throughout his life struggled against poverty. Originally trained for the priesthood, he abandoned this in favour of writing. He had already achieved a reputation as a controversial writer when the bookseller Le Breton invited him to become the editor of a proposed encyclopaedia in French. The idea was inspired by the success of the first English encyclopaedia in 1728, and its aim was to produce in one set of books a summary of all the knowledge men possessed at the time. However, Le Breton's plan for a modest factual work was changed out of all recognition by Diderot. It proved to be an enormous undertaking, and the first volume did not appear until 1751. Even this volume suffered from the resignation of Diderot's co-editor, D'Alembert, and the considerable censoring of articles by Le Breton who was anxious to avoid persecution.

The problem was that Diderot had in mind something far more ambitious than Le Breton. He managed to persuade nearly all the great writers, including Montesquieu, Voltaire and Rousseau, to contribute, along with some well-known figures in the world of politics, such as Mirabeau, Necker and Turgot. This was the only work on which nearly all the French *philosophes* collaborated, and in this sense it symbolises the Enlightenment. As volume succeeded volume – there were 28 volumes in all, including 11 of illustrations, and the work was not completed until 1772 – it became clear that the *Encyclopédie* was far more than just a work of information.

* Although the writers often disagreed with each other, there was an important common theme running through the work – that man was a rational being who was capable of finding out the truth about himself and the world without relying on religion to supply the answers. The authors were particularly hostile to the Roman Catholic Church's claim to have a monopoly of knowledge, which they consciously set out to end. Diderot was not himself anti-religious, but aimed to 'liberate God' from the shackles of the Church. He said that the purpose of the work was that 'by becoming better informed we may become happier and more virtuous'. This optimistic belief that education and knowledge led to wisdom and improved morals was crucial to Diderot's philosophy.

Diderot had no clear political ideas. He believed that government was there for the benefit of the people, but that ordinary people had no right to oppose laws, even bad laws. Clearly he had no difficulty reconciling himself to the style of government adopted by Catherine II and other Enlightened Despots. On the other hand he opposed Louis XV's attempts to increase his powers at the expense of the *parlements* in the 1770s. Along with the other *philosophes* he was quick to condemn despotism in his own country whilst condoning it when it came from monarchs who patronised his books. He could also be vague about his religious beliefs, stating once that 'I am a Christian because it is reasonable to be so'. He was anxious to popularise recent scientific discoveries, which he saw as the key to liberating mankind from superstition. He even put forward his own theory of evolution which he was, however, unable to prove.

* The book was a best-seller, despite its high price, and had some surprising supporters. Although officially condemned and banned both by the Church and Louis XV's government (the latter arguing that 'it tended to destroy royal authority and to encourage a spirit of independence and revolt') it was protected by the patronage of people such as the government minister Malesherbes – nominally responsible for enforcing the ban – and Madame de Pompadour, Louis XV's mistress, who even contributed an article on 'rouge' herself. Diderot was also helped

by the support of Catherine II, who gave him money when he was again in poverty, and who invited him to Russia to discuss politics. The work did much to popularise the ideas of the *philosophes* and may have contributed to the climate of religious toleration which was becoming widespread. It has also been argued that its clear descriptions of manufacturing processes, helped by the excellent quality of the diagrams, encouraged more people to set up their own workshops and start using machinery and that in this way he helped further undermine the power of the guilds in their losing fight to maintain monopolies over manufacturing for their own members.

Diderot wrote much else, and was for a long time the art critic for an influential magazine, arguing strongly for art that was useful and denouncing the romantic paintings of the fashionable Boucher. Yet the *Encyclopédie* remains his greatest monument. Through a lifetime's work he was able to overcome the problems of production, the opposition of the government, the censorship of his publisher and the squabbling amongst his 200 contributors.

Believing that it was possible for mankind to perfect itself through knowledge, Diderot offered reason and knowledge as replacements for absolute monarchy and religious supersition. This optimistic philosophy was criticised by Voltaire (amongst others) in his own lifetime. Yet despite mankind's failure to become wise and moral through reading his volumes, Diderot's achievements are undeniable. The *Encyclopédie* was the manifesto of the Enlightenment and played a major part in making the new philosophy acceptable to educated French people.

3 Voltaire

Voltaire was the greatest writer of the eighteenth century and one of the greatest in the history of Europe. For nearly 60 years the words poured from the pen of this most prolific writer of his age. His works range from letters to his friends to poems, plays, serious historical works, novels and satires. Today he is best remembered for his one-line epigrams – no dictionary of quotations would be complete without them – and his brilliant satire *Candide*, which should be read by every student of eighteenth-century history. In his lifetime he was admired and fêted by the respectable society he liked to criticise, and could count both Frederick II and Catherine II as his friends. Yet this most influential and popular of the *philosophes* had few original ideas and, unlike Montesquieu or Rousseau, was never able to offer an alternative to the existing systems of government.

Voltaire was the pen-name for Françoise Marie Arouet (1694–1778), the son of a lawyer. Originally trained for the law himself, he quickly abandoned this for writing. At first he was a humorous writer, but his work became more serious after he suffered a beating and imprisonment in the Bastille for offending the powerful Duc de Rohan. Another important influence was his visit to England between 1726 and 1728. Like Montesquieu he came to admire the political and literary freedom that the English enjoyed.

From the 1730s until his death he was the most famous writer in France. The government varied in its attitude towards him, sometimes banning his works when they became too critical, and at other times, as when Madame de Pompadour held sway over the French court, encouraging his writing. For much of his life he lived at Ferney, conveniently close to the Swiss border should he need to go into exile. Here he acquired a great deal of wealth, much of it from financial speculation and some from the slave trade, and ruled as a benevolent Lord of the Manor to the local peasants, ensuring they all paid their dues to him, but providing them with a new church. Sixty servants looked after him; not for Voltaire the poverty of Diderot and Rousseau. In 1778 he was allowed to return to Paris after 28 years. He was greeted with enormous crowds and enthusiasm but he died soon after.

* Voltaire's works attacked superstition and oppression. He was at his best when dealing with cases of religious intolerance and abuses of the law. His campaigns to clear the names of the Protestant Calas, executed by the *Parlement* on trumped up murder charges, and of the young Chevalier de la Barre, similarly executed for sacrilege, made his name in Europe. In both cases he was able through a relentless pamphlet campaign to force a reluctant government to concede that the convictions had been wrong and to award some compensation to the widow of Calas. He was cynical about the existence of God – one of his most famous epigrams was 'If God did not exist it would be necessary to invent Him' – and a bitter opponent of the power, wealth, privilege and intolerance of the Roman Catholic Church. Not surprisingly the Church banned the faithful from reading his books and refused him a Christian burial, although he did claim to be a believer.

* At first Voltaire shared the optimistic philosophy of Diderot. He contributed to the *Encyclopédie* and produced his own works popularising recent scientific discoveries. However, his faith in progress was lost as a result of the Lisbon Earthquake of 1755 in which many thousands of ordinary people died. The result was *Candide* (1759), his most famous book. Candide, the innocent hero of the book, absorbs the fashionable optimistic theories of his teacher Dr Pangloss and wanders round the world in search of his long-lost love. This gave Voltaire the opportunity to poke fun at everything he disliked, not least Candide's naive faith in the goodness of man. In this extract Voltaire satirises eighteenth-century warfare in general, and his patron Frederick II (thinly disguised as 'The King of Bulgaria') in particular.

1 the two blue-coats put Candide in irons and led him off to their
  regiment. He was taught to right turn, left turn, draw his
  rammer, receive his rammer, present, fire, double quick march

and received thirty strokes with the cane. Next day he drilled a little less badly and received only twenty strokes. On the third day he received the admiration of his comrades by receiving only ten.

Candide was bewildered and could not see how he was a hero. One fine day he decided to go for a walk – nowhere in particular – on the principle that human beings, like animals, have the right to use their legs as they wish. He had not gone six miles when he was overtaken by four other heroes who tied him up and carried him to prison.

At the court-martial Candide was asked if he preferred to run the gauntlet thirty-six times or have his skull split by a dozen bullets. It was no use he saying that he didn't want either. So, exercising that divine gift known as 'Free Will', he chose to run the gauntlet.

After two of these canters Candide gave up and asked them, as a favour, to blow his brains out. This favour was graciously granted, and he was told to kneel down. At that moment the King of Bulgaria happened to pass by and asked what the culprit had done. Being told, and being a monarch of genius, he realised that Candide was simply an unworldly philosopher and pardoned him.

In three weeks the King of Bulgaria was at war with the King of Abaria. The two armies were unequalled for their smartness, equipment and tactics. Their cannon made a music never heard in hell itself. To start with the artillery laid low about six thousand men on either side. After that muskets rid this best of all possible worlds of some nine to ten thousand of the scum. Finally the bayonet killed thousands more. At length, when the Kings ordered the *Te Deum* to be sung in both camps, Candide decided to go elsewhere.

Passing over the heaps of dead he came to a village. It was in ashes, having been an Abarian village and burnt, in accordance with the rules of war, by the Bulgars. Old men mangled by bayonets watched their wives and children dying. Amongst the dying were girls who had been used to satisy the heroes' natural needs. As fast as he could Candide made off to another village. This was Bulgarian and the Abarian heroes had treated it the same way.

---

* Voltaire's attitude towards government was unclear. Although he could bitterly denounce the abuse of power by royal tyrants as effectively as the other writers, he also showed his admiration for strong kings through his flattering biographies of Louis XIV and Charles XII of Swden. He was in favour of absolute monarchy – 'No government can be effective unless it possesses absolute power' – and was appalled by the idea of giving the ordinary people any say in running the state –

A statue of Voltaire dressed as a classical thinker

'Once the people begin to reason, all is lost. I abominate the idea of government by the masses'. At other times he casually referred to the ordinary people as *canaille* (rabble). He was in favour of the state providing an education system, but not that it should be extended to the poor. Instead he supported the idea of an absolute monarch, supported by an élite of educated nobles. Such a monarch would rule justly and wisely, establish religious toleration and reduce the powers and wealth of the established church. He would establish a free press, give people equality under the law, and abolish feudal dues.

It is easy to point out the inconsistencies in Voltaire's beliefs. He bitterly attacked the churches, yet made sure his own peasants worshipped in one; he denounced religious intolerance, yet was himself prejudiced against both Catholicism and Judaism; the writer who so scathingly attacked the meaningless and destructive wars of the period in *Candide* did not hesitate to profit from them personally; the man who denounced feudal dues made sure that he always received his from the peasants; he attacked tyrannical government but had his closest relationships with Frederick and Catherine rather than with his own easy-going monarch.

Despite all this, his greatness remains. With wit and style he undermined the *ancien régime*. His defence of Calas is a milestone in the history of religious toleration. He destroyed the self-confidence of the upper classes and by his success encouraged others to criticise in turn. As Louis David, artist and French revolutionary of the 1790s put it, 'He taught us to be free'. It was an epitaph Voltaire would have liked.

4 Rousseau

Jean-Jacques Rousseau (1712–78) was the most enigmatic and solitary of the *philosophes*, but the one whose ideas have had the most lasting impact on the modern world. The son of a French Protestant living in Geneva, he ran away from home at the age of 16 and spent the rest of his life moving round Europe restlessly. He had few friends and treated them badly. According to his disarmingly honest *Confessions*, published in the 1780s after his death, he admitted to being a thief and to having fathered and then abandoned, a number of illegitimate children, although there is no proof that what he claimed here was true.

In common with other *philosophes*, he contributed to the *Encyclopédie* and wrote pamphlets on a wide variety of subjects, including science, music and the theatre. Typically, he quarrelled with the editors of the *Encyclopédie* and subsequently tried to have its publication prevented. His fame rests on three books all written within five years of each other – *La Nouvelle Héloïse* (1759), *Émile* (1762) and *The Social Contract* also of 1762.

 * The first of these was a romantic novel about the doomed love affair between a poor man and the daughter of a noble. The book was a

best-seller, particularly amongst women, and may be said to have been the first such romance, establishing a type of fiction whose popularity shows no signs of declining. *Nouvelle Héloïse* was also delivering a clear message; that human beings are not simply governed by reason and scientific laws, as the Newtonians argued, but by emotions as well. In addition the novel, by implication, denounced a society where birth and social conventions counted for more than feelings for one another. This appeal to the emotions was always a significant part of Rousseau's arguments. He rejected the rationality that underlined much of eighteenth-century thought. He is often credited (wrongly) with the concept of 'Back to Nature' and the 'Noble Savage'. This was the idea, which Rousseau certainly did much to popularise, that in their original state people had lived simple and decent lives until civilisation began. Inequalities of wealth, social disorder and crime were the result of the creation of governments, laws and economic progress. But Rousseau never argued that it was possible to return to the idyllic existence he thought early man had enjoyed, although he did wish to limit the restraints civilisation and laws placed on people's lives. In the seventeenth century the influential English philosopher Hobbes had justified absolute monarchy on the grounds that before governments had been invented men's lives had been 'nasty, brutish and short'. He argued that early man had been uncivilised and barbaric, and that civilisation and government was for everyone's benefit. Now Rousseau was arguing the opposite, and by doing so laid open to question why governments were required at all.

   * *Émile* represents a milestone in the history of education. Émile is the boy who receives an ideal education. He has a single teacher who looks after him until he is 20. Up until this time it was generally believed that children were born sinful, and that they had quickly to be taught right and wrong, by force if necessary. Indeed, there was scarcely any concept of childhood at all. Children were seen as miniature adults and were expected to dress, behave and work like their parents as quickly as possible. Rousseau argued that children are born without sin, but can be corrupted by cruel parents and civilisation. It is interesting to contrast this with the way Rousseau later claimed to have dealt with his own children. Children should be allowed to develop freely, with the minimum of restraints and at their own pace; they should not, for example, be taught to read and write until they wished to do so themselves. Turning the traditional role of the teacher on its head, Rousseau argued that his job was 'not to teach truth and virtue' but merely to prevent 'vice and error'. He created the idea of child-centred education, even if some of his ideas, such as having one teacher for every child, were and are totally unrealistic. In his own lifetime the Polish government tried to introduce some of his ideas into their schools, but they did not become widely read until the nineteenth century. Yet in the long run they have had an immense influence. Not

only did he found the idea of progressive child-centred education, but in many respects he helped invent the idea that there is such a thing as childhood – a separate phase of people's lives when they are and should be treated differently from adults.

    * In *The Social Contract* Rousseau turned to politics. This relatively short book starts with a ringing declaration – 'Man is born free but is everywhere in chains'. He then went on to look at why it was that governments and rulers exist, and whether it was possible to create a system of government which could combine man's desire for freedom with the necessity of laws, governments and civlisation. His solution was the Social Contract. This was not, of course, a new idea, but Rousseau developed Locke's ideas in an original way. He totally opposed the idea of parliaments, and was probably the only *philosophe* who had no admiration for the English system of government. To him electing a representative meant that men gave up their freedom and rights to a handful of people whose only concern was their own power and interests. Only direct participation by all citizens could ensure that all people maintained their rights. This view makes him unique amongst eighteenth-century writers, and ensured that none of the Enlightened Despots would seek to curry his favour. Rousseau realised that mass meetings could never work in large states, and for this reason advocated his system only in small city-states like Geneva. It is significant that when the Polish government asked his advice on reforming their constitution in the 1770s, he suggested only modest reforms, nothing like the ones in *Social Contract*.

    Rousseau's greatest problem was in devising a system whereby the government acted in the best interests of the citizens, even where there was no agreement amongst them. In his view even a democracy was unsatisfactory, since there was no certainty that what the majority of people wanted was, in fact, in the best interests of the community as a whole. Instead he put forward the concept of the General Will, which presumed the existence of a community that would be willing to act unselfishly and support an idea, even if it only enjoyed minority support, if it was seen that it would benefit the community. Bad laws could not then be passed since nobody would benefit from them. In this extract Rousseau explains why the General Will can never be wrong:

1 So long as men joined together consider themselves a single body, they only have one will which is directed towards their common preservation and general well-being. Then all the forces of the state are vigorous and simple and its principles clear. It has no
5 incompatible or conflicting interests. The common good makes itself so evident that only common sense is needed to dicern it. Upright and simple men are difficult to deceive because of their simplicity. When we see amongst the happiest people in the world peasants regulating the affairs of state under an oak tree and

10 always acting wisely, can we help feeling contempt for the
refinements of other nations?
   A state thus governed needs few laws, and whenever there is a
need for a new law, that need is universally seen. The first man to
propose the law is only giving voice to what everyone feels. Each
15 has already resolved to do it as soon as he is sure all the others will
do the same.

The concept of the General Will raised many problems. Not the least
of these was his assertion that if necessary the General Will could be
forced on the people, since it was in everyone's long-term interest. A
minority, representing the General Will, could 'Force men to be free' –
an interesting concept, which might appear a contradiction in terms –
and people refusing to accept the General Will could be banished or, in
extreme cases, executed.

Rousseau's book is not only a plea for direct participatory democracy, but could also be used to justify the most ruthless dictatorship. In
the last 150 years many dictators have done evil in the name of a belief
or ideology which was forced on people on the grounds that the ruler
knew better than his people what was in their best interests. In
Rousseau's lifetime these views had little impact, although during the
French Revolution, Robespierre did try to introduce a system of
government based on the General Will. Its association with the
guillotine and its collapse within a year discredited any further attempts
to copy Rousseau directly.

* Nevertheless, his long term impact, both on the development of
democracy and of dictatorship, has been considerable. In his lifetime he
certainly helped popularise the romantic movement throughout educated society. When Queen Marie-Antoinette created her fairytale
Hameau (Hamlet) in the grounds of Versailles where she and her
friends could dress up as peasants, milk real cows and have picnics by a
lake, she was reflecting the new fashion for a simple back-to-nature life.
Rousseau questioned the whole idea of civilisation as progress and
created the romantic novel. As the writer who gave a moral justification
for democracy he stands apart from all the other writers who either
favoured absolute monarchy, or a limited participation by richer people
in government. He was the most important of all the *philosophes*.

Other Writers

The *philosophes* were not a united group of writers. In fact they agreed
on very little. Their coming together for the *Encyclopédie* was not
typical; more typical was the way in which they squabbled over it.
What they did hold in common was a belief that there should be
freedom of publication, that the Church should lose its monopoly over
education, that people should be free to practise their own religions

freely, and that government existed to benefit the people. There were, of course, many others who wrote on politics and economics other than the famous *philosophes* discussed earlier in this chapter. Amongst these were British authors, including Adam Smith, who, in his *Wealth of Nations* (1776), advocated the ending of government control over commerce and the establishment of free trade. A number of German writers likewise helped to popularise enlightened ideas in their states. Nevertheless it was the French writers discussed earlier who were the most influential. They were the only ones to be read widely outside their own lands.

　* Of the Italian writers, Cesare Beccaria was the most important. His book *Crime and Punishment* was published in 1764 when the author was 26. Developing Montesquieu's criticisms of penal policy, Beccaria suggested a totally new attitude towards the prevention and punishment of crime, and started a debate on the best way to deal with criminals which shows no signs of abating today.

1　Every act of authority of one man over another, for which there is not absolute necessity, is tyrannical.

　　Justice is the bond which is necessary to keep the interests of individuals united, and without which men would return to
5　barbarity. All punishments which exceed this necessity are unjust.

　　Crimes can only be measured by the injury done to society. Can torture reverse the crime he has committed?

　　The aim of punishment is, therefore, to prevent the criminal
10　from doing further injury to society, and to prevent others from commiting a similar offence.

　　All trials should be in public. Secret accusations are an abuse, but are custom in nations with weak governments. This custom makes men false and treacherous.
15　The punishment of a noble should in no way differ from that of the lowest member of society.

　　Crimes are prevented by the certainty, not the severity, of punishment. If punishments are severe, men will perpetrate other crimes, to avoid the punishment due to the first.
20　There is no right to punish by death.

　　It is better to prevent crimes than to punish them.

　　Would you prevent crimes? Let laws be clear and simple. They must not favour a particular class of men. Let the laws be feared, and the laws only. The fear of men is a fatal source of crime. Men
25　enslaved are more cruel and debauched than those who are free. Let liberty be attended with knowledge.

　　A punishment must not be an act of violence. It should be public, necessary and immediate and the least possible proportional to the crime and determined by the laws.

His arguments had a considerable influence on Catherine II, who incorporated many of his statements into her *Nakaz*, and other rulers took steps to liberalise their penal codes in later years. Beccaria never repeated the success of his first book, which was one of the few works with a direct impact on the policies of several rulers. He freely admitted his debt to earlier *philosophes*, particularly Montesquieu, and this demonstrates how their example inspired others to develop their ideas.

    * A group of writers who also enjoyed a definite but limited influence on the policies of some states at this time were known as the Physiocrats. Their most prominent member was Quesnay, who wrote his *Tableau Economique* in 1758, but they also included Turgot who was for a short time Controller of Finances under Louis XVI. Developing the idea that nature should rule, these writers argued for minimum state interference in the economy – the idea of *laissez-faire*, which contradicted the previously widely-held view of the mercantalists that the monarch should discharge imports through high duties and encourage exports so as to build up a nation's gold reserves. The Physiocrats wanted to see industry and trade freed from government regulations and the control of guilds alike. There should be no internal customs duties as these discouraged trade. Serfdom should be abolished. All this would lead to an increase in population – something that all the *philosophes* felt was desirable in order to stimulate the economy, and necessary because they thought (quite wrongly) that the population of Europe was then in decline. They also advocated the replacement of the existing myriad of taxes and dues with a single land tax. This would simplify the tax system, be fairer in that the wealthy Landlord would pay more than the peasant, and tax the real basis of the state's wealth – the land. For some time the Physiocrats had considerable influence, as Turgot's appointment suggests. They drew attention to an area of society, economics, which other writers tended either to neglect or to take for granted. Their suggestion that land rather than gold was the true basis of judging a nation's wealth was a step in the right direction, if over-simple in an age when trade and industry were growing in importance, and their tax suggestions would have gone a long way towards putting into practice the theory of removing the privileges of the wealthy.

    The reality was different. Turgot aroused great opposition from privileged groups when he tried to put Physiocratic ideas into practice, and was quickly dismissed by his timid monarch; and even where a land tax was introduced, as in Baden in Germany, it created as many problems as it solved. However, the idea that the state should give complete freedom to merchants and industrialists did take root, and this was later to help lead to the great expansion of industry and trade that took place in Europe in the nineteenth century.

    During the eighteenth century rulers were faced with a mass of advice from writers eager to gain patronage and to put forward reforms on a wide variety of topics. Some monarchs ignored the advice and ruled without changing their ways. A few did take up the views of the writers, at least in theory, and started to adapt their countries in line with the suggestions made. How well they were able to put theory into practice will be looked at in the following chapters.

Making notes on 'The Writers of the Enlightenment'

Your notes should give you an understanding of (i) who the main *philosophes* were, and what they believed in. They should also provide

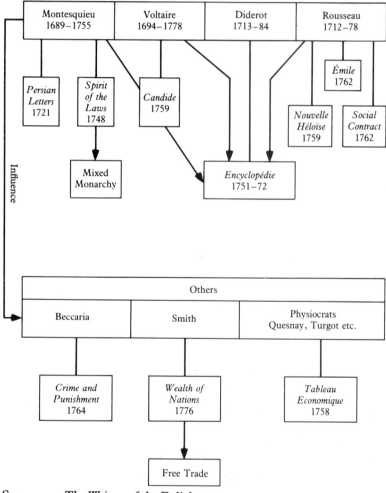

Summary – The Writers of the Enlightenment

you with some awareness of (ii) what the enlightened writers agreed upon and what caused disagreement among them, and with an understanding of (iii) the reasons for the hostility between the Catholic Church and the writers. Finally you will have some understanding of (iv) the importance and influence of the writers, although you will not have fully mastered this area until you have discovered in the later chapters the extent to which monarchs were willing to put these ideas into practice.

If you are an experienced note-maker, you will be able to make satisfactory notes using four headings derived from the previous paragraph. If you are less experienced you may find the following headings helpful.

1   Montesquieu
1.1. His background and early influences
1.2. *Lettres Persanes* – ideas and importance
1.3. *De l'Esprit des Lois*
      a) Mixed monarchy – how it would work
      b) Influence and significance of *De l'Esprit des Lois*
2   Diderot and the *Encyclopédie*
2.1. Origins of the *Encyclopédie*
2.2. Religious and political ideas
2.3. Influence of the book
3   Voltaire
3.1. Life and influences
3.2. Attitude towards religion
3.3. *Candide*
3.4. Attitude towards government
4   Rousseau
4.1. His background and early influences
4.2. *Nouvelle Héloïse*
      a) Ideas
      b) Importance
4.3. *Émile*
      a) Ideas
      b) Importance
4.4   *Social Contract*
      a) The idea of the General Will
      b) The social Contract as the foundation of modern democracy
      c) The Social Contract as the foundation of modern dictatorship
4.5. His influence and importance
5   Other Writers
5.1. What united them?
5.2. The ideas and significance of Beccaria
5.3. The ideas and significance of the Physiocrats

Answering essay questions on 'The Writers of the Enlightenment'

A-level examiners rarely set descriptive or narrative questions. You can, therefore, expect all questions to be analytical in approach. This means that you will be asked a specific question about a topic (rather than being invited to write all you know about it!). You will need to identify the key points on which the examiner is focusing and construct an answer (in the form of an 'argument') around them. The 'facts' will be your evidence to support your argument. Evidence and argument should be combined in each paragraph. Try to avoid the common mistake of writing a narrative account in the first part of the essay and then switching to discussion and opinion at the end. The two should always be combined.

Questions which contrast the theory of the enlightened writers with the practice of eighteenth-century monarchies are common in the examination. You will not be able to answer such essays until you have completed this book. Relatively few essays ask solely about the influence of the writers. You are likely to be asked to discuss either (i) The aims and methods of the writers, (ii) The work and importance of one (or two) writers; these might be either named for you by the examiner, or you might be invited to select your own examples, or (iii) The reasons for the hostility between the Catholic Church and the writers.

Some questions asked on this topic are relatively straightforward, such as:

1. 'In what ways did the thinkers of the Enlightenment seek to improve society?'
2. 'Assess the importance of Rousseau in the Enlightenment.'

A basic answer for question 1 would involve a series of paragraphs outlining the main ideas of the writers. Which paragraph points would you include if you used this approach? A more sophisticated approach would be to concentrate on the phrase 'seek to improve society'. Here you would link the specific ideas of the writers with their vision of a better society. What extra points would you need to include if you used this approach?

Question 2 can also be answered on two levels. On a basic level it requires an assessment of Rousseau's ideas and the impact these had on Europe. Which paragraph headings would you include? A higher quality answer would also assess his significance by comparing his impact with that of the other writers. What criteria would you use to decide how Rousseau's importance compares with that of other writers?

Sometimes the examiner will ask you to concentrate on just one aspect of the Enlightenment such as the hostility towards the Catholic

Church. A typical example is:

3. 'Why did the Catholic Church attract the disapproval of the *philosophes*?'

The first word gives the clue as to the sort of essay question this is. The key word 'why' indicates that the examiner is looking for the reasons for the hostility. The essay *assumes* that there was hostility, but you might wish to discuss how valid this assumption is in your introductory paragraph. You might then go on to look at the reasons for this hostility, dealing with one major cause in each paragraph. You might now find it helpful to prepare an essay plan for this question, by carrying out the following steps:

a) List the points you would briefly make in your introductory paragraph to establish that there was hostility between the Church and the writers. Be careful not to be carried away with this. Remember that this is the introduction to your answer, not the answer itself.

b) List six paragraph headings, each providing a reason for this hostility. Each heading will probably begin with the word 'because'.

c) Identify one or more generalisations (you can build these by amalgamating two or more of your paragraph headings) that you would wish to stress in your conclusion.

Source-based questions on 'The Writers of the Enlightenment'

1 Voltaire
Read the extracts from *Candide* on pages 15–16, and also study the picture of the statue of Voltaire on page 17. Answer the following questions.

a) What does the extract from *Candide* tell us about Voltaire's attitude to (i) warfare, military discipline and soldiers in the eighteenth century, and (ii) religion? You should support your answers with appropriate quotations from the source. (8 marks)

b) *Candide* is a work of fiction. How far does this affect its value as evidence about eighteenth-century military practices? (4 marks)

c) What was Voltaire's purpose in writing this book? (3 marks)

d) The statue of Voltaire is designed to create an impression of the sort of person he was. What is this impression? (2 marks)

e) To what extent does the written extract (i) support, and (ii) contradict the impression given in the statue of the sort of person Voltaire was? (3 marks)

2 Rousseau and Beccaria

Read the extracts from *Social Contract* on pages 20–1 and *On Punishment* on page 22, and then answer the following questions.

a) How does the extract from *Social Contract* explain Rousseau's attitude to the need for laws?   (4 marks)

b) What does Beccaria say are (i) the causes of crime, (ii) the best way to prevent crimes, and (iii) the purpose of punishment?

    (6 marks)

c) Compare and contrast the attitudes of Beccaria and Rousseau towards laws and crime.   (4 marks)

d) Beccaria's suggestions for law reforms were often adopted by eighteenth-century monarchs, while Rousseau's were not. Suggest reasons why this was so.   (6 marks)

CHAPTER 3

Frederick the Great

1 The New King

When Frederick II ascended the throne in 1740, most foreign observers expected a new era of enlightenment to flourish in the scattered lands which made up Prussia. In the previous few years Crown Prince Frederick had established a formidable reputation as a thinker, writer, musician and lover of all that was best in literature and philosophy. The English ambassador confidently predicted a halving of the size of the huge Prussian army, while in France there were rumours that the new king would appoint Voltaire as his Chief Minister.

Within weeks all these high hopes were to be shattered when Frederick sent his troops in an unprovoked attack on neighbouring Austria, so unleashing 23 years of war on Germany and on Europe. Frederick proved to be one of the most formidable military commanders of the eighteenth century, yet maintained his reputation as an Enlightened Despot and Philosopher-King. His dazzling achievements at home and abroad were to influence generations of future leaders of Germany down to Adolf Hitler. He is arguably the most influential king in Germany's history.

* Historians have been fascinated by Frederick's childhood and the influence it had on his later policies. His father, Frederick William I, ruled Prussia single-handedly from 1713–40. The latter's reputation has suffered in comparison to that of his more interesting and ostensibly successful son, but his reign was immensely important for the development of Prussia. When Frederick William I ascended the throne his lands, scattered over North Germany, ranged from the feudal province of East Prussia where proud *Junker* noble families lorded over their serfs, to the tiny but more advanced provinces of Cleves, Mark and Ravensburg (see map on page 31). By the end of his reign he had welded these together into a unitary state ruled over by the monarch. He exercised tight personal control over every aspect of political life in Prussia, never allowed his ministers any personal power, and spent months each year personally visiting his provinces, spying and inspecting the work of every government department. He gave Prussia a centralised system of government, reformed the finances, and started a system of primary schools. He also built up the army to a formidable 80000 strong, created an efficient and flexible system of conscription and training, and equipped his soldiers with the finest weapons. At a time when success in battle depended on discipline and the speed at which men marched, Frederick William's troops were the best in Europe.

It was an army he hardly ever used. This most militaristic of kings carefully avoided wars, which were not only risky and expensive, but offended against his strict moral code. The fact that he rarely used his fine army, combined with his fondness for exceptionally tall soldiers, led him to be treated as a joke by other European rulers. The stories abounded about how he would sign a treaty in exchange for a few giants, and how his agents scoured Europe seeking new recruits of suitable size for his Regiment of Giants. Whilst other kings fought wars for prestige, built palaces and copied the elaborate court customs of Versailles, Frederick William avoided wars and lived with his family in a few rooms in one modest palace. It was not an image designed to impress the rest of Europe.

Frederick William's militarisation of Prussia certainly helped weld together an otherwise totally artificial country. His achievements in government and finance were to give Frederick II a launch pad from which to turn Prussia into a Great Power. Eventually Frederick came to appreciate just how much he owed to his unusual father. Unlike many historians, he never underestimated what Frederick William had done to develop his country. The strange relationship between father and son was in many ways the most important legacy that Frederick William left.

* There is no doubt that Frederick William treated his son with cruelty. Frederick was born in 1712, just before his father became King. It was clear that from an early age father and son had little in common. Frederick William saw himself as a simple Prussian soldier. He had no intellectual pretensions and he despised people who were well educated. His interests were solely connected with his duties – to supervise the government, to make the laws and to drill the soldiers. His only relaxations were smoking, drinking and exchanging jokes with army officers.

Frederick was quite different. He showed considerable interest in the arts and literature. This may have been partly an inheritance from his mother, Sophia Dorothea, the sister of George I of England, or from the encouragement of his early governess and tutor. His father ensured that by the age of five he knew all the steps of the Prussian drill, but before long he was also playing the flute, writing love poems – in French, a language he always preferred to his own – and reading in secret those books of classical literature which his father had banned as being irrelevant and dangerous for a King of Prussia.

Frederick William was appalled. It seemed as if all his hard work would be thrown away. The King bullied and shouted at his wayward son. A trivial incident, such as Frederick wearing gloves in cold weather, could spark off another tantrum from the King. For years Frederick, a sensitive, intelligent and cultured boy, had to endure the insults, shouts and beatings of his coarse and crude father. It was the historian Thomas Carlyle in the 1840s who first built up the picture of the unfeeling father who terrorised and brutalised his talented son,

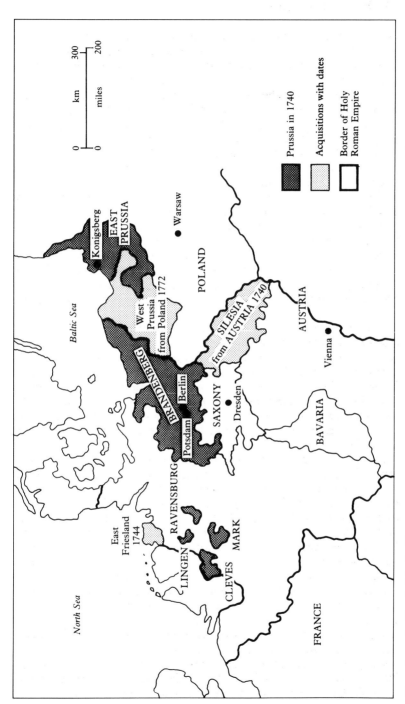

Prussia under Frederick the Great

resulting in a coarsening of his character. This now seems an oversim-
plified picture. Because of his father's frequent trips to the provinces,
Frederick was left alone to enjoy his music and books for months on
end. In addition it seems that Frederick and his elder sister Wilhelmina
rather enjoyed teasing their father by deliberately doing or saying what
most angered him. Nancy Mitford points out in her sympathetic
biography of Frederick that 'if he was beaten and humiliated it was to a
large extent his own fault'.

If it were partly a game on Frederick's part, it lost its humour in
1730. The 18-year-old Prince conspired with his friend Lieutenant
Katte to run away from home and escape to France or England where
they could be free. It was an amateurish plot and was easily discovered
by the King. This time his fury was uncontrollable. Frederick had
defied the King and had tried to desert from the army. With his simple
principles, Frederick William saw these as unforgivable sins. As he
believed that a just King should treat his own children in the same way
as his other subjects, Frederick was imprisoned and forced to watch the
execution of Katte from his cell window. He was himself threatened
with execution, and it was only international pressure which persuaded
Frederick William to relent. For a short time Frederick was deprived of
his position as Crown Prince and was kept under tight supervision.

Frederick's reaction to this disaster was to learn how to lie. He
pretended to be contrite and begged to be allowed to learn how to be
King the right way. He even agreed to marry a princess, Elizabeth-
Christine of Brunswick-Bevern, whom he did not like. 'Thank God it's
over' he wrote to his sister after the wedding day. Despite his strong
objections to the marriage, Frederick had submitted to the wishes of his
father. In the same way he eagerly accepted his new duties as a junior
army officer and civil servant. He was sent on a tour of inspection to
East Prussia and watched his first military campaign with the famous
Prince Eugene in 1734. The more he took his duties seriously, the more
his father relaxed the controls and thought that perhaps his son would
make a successful king after all.

It is easy to see this as sheer hypocrisy from Frederick, who now
realised he could not actually beat his father and would have to follow
his wishes until he died. In fact he found his new education more useful
than he had expected. He discovered, to his surprise, that he was
actually interested in watching a military campaign and seeing how the
country was run. It is not unreasonable to argue that this really was a
long overdue part of Frederick's education. It is doubtful whether a
king who knew everything about French literature and nothing about
administration would have been a successful monarch, Frederick
William may have been a bully, but he was right to think that culture
alone would make a poor king.

The years from 1736–40 were the happiest of Frederick's life. He was
now allowed to live in his own palace at Rheinsburg. At last he was free

to resume his reading and music. He surrounded himself with like-minded young men. Literature and philosophy could be read and discussed until late at night. It was at this time that Frederick started his mutually flattering correspondence with Voltaire, already the most famous writer in France. During these years Frederick read widely and was interested in a range of subjects. This education, combined with the more practical lessons his father insisted on, resulted in an unusually well educated monarch: the Philosopher-King combined with the man of action. It was also during these years that he started writing himself.

* His first book was written in 1737. It was called *Considerations on the Present Political Condition of Europe*, and was based on his readings rather than any first-hand experience. In fact, Frederick, for all his protestations about the value of travel, never once left Germany. Most of his observations were uncontroversial – Holland had declined to a country of cheese-makers, whilst Britain and France were destined to continue to quarrel over colonies and trade. He did observe that Austrian power was in decline and that the death of Charles VI might see this exposed.

A more famous book was his *Antimachiavel*, written in 1739 but not published until shortly after he became king. Here he denounced the political philosophy of Machiavelli. On the face of it, this was a strong plea for kings to be honest and put the interests of their subjects first. Monarchs should not fear their own subjects. They should set standards and act as the First Servant of the State. They should protect the innocent and look after the poor. Honesty and truth were the principles by which a king should rule. No wonder Europe hailed the coming of the Philosopher-King in 1740. However, in reality the message of the book was more ambiguous than it appeared. Whereas in his *Considerations* of 1737 Frederick had argued that it was always 'unjust' to attack lands to which a king had no legal claim, *Antimachiavel* is by no means so clear. Here Frederick justified not only wars fought in self-defence, but also wars

1 by which a ruler maintains rights. Kings are subject to no court of law, and so their rights must be decided by the sword . . . there are also aggressive wars which carry justification; these are the preventative wars which princes have good reason to undertake.

The same book argued strongly for an absolute monarchy, for only under such a system could a king have the freedom to help his people. And in one telling phrase Frederick wrote 'It is a political error to practice deceit – *if deceit is carried too far*'. All in all it would seem that *Antimachiavel* was not so much a denunciation of Machiavelli, but a machiavellian adaptation of the writer for eighteenth-century use.

* Frederick William had once despaired of his effeminate son with

his head in the clouds, full of woolly ideas and unrealistic ideals. In reality it seems that from an early age Frederick had combined intellect with clear aims and ambitions, and was quite ready to sacrifice the former for the latter. As early as 1726, when it was feared his father might die from one of the numerous illnesses which plagued him throughout his life, the 14-year-old Crown Prince was coolly discussing what policies he would follow as King. In 1731, in one of his earliest statements of ideas, written when he was still in prison and with little hope, it seemed, of ever being allowed to become King, he wrote that Prussia must choose her destiny. One option was to live in peace with her neighbours – the policy his father practised – always on the defensive and always vulnerable to seeing her scattered provinces picked off by larger powers. The alternative – the one Frederick favoured – was aggressive war against neighbours to conquer land, unite the scattered provinces, and turn Prussia into a real power. He argued this was justified, so long as the king of the new, powerful Prussia looked after his people.

Intellectual or warrior? Frederick saw no reason to have to choose between the two. He would conquer land but also look after his people. The end justified the means, Frederick William would have been proud of his son; they were not really so different after all.

2 The Philosopher-King

Frederick's first acts on ascending the throne early in 1740 seemed to confirm that a new progressive era was about to start in Prussia. A stream of popular decrees was enacted during the first few weeks of his reign. He ordered ministers to put the interests of the people as their first priority; he abolished most types of torture and the cruel forms of execution; he lightened press censorship (giving Prussia, for a time, the freest press in Europe); he banned the sadistic initiation ceremonies endured by new recruits to the army, and he limited the nobility's right to hunt over other people's land. He re-established the Academy of Science, with the Frenchman Maupertius as its President, and started work on an opera house. He consulted the merchants on how to stimulate trade and took the first steps to establish state granaries to help stabilise the price of grain. He decreed full religious toleration, extending this even to Muslims, although whether there were any in Prussia to benefit from this is doubtful. 'Everyone can go to heaven in their own way' he declared, neatly summing up the ideal of religious toleration.

* It was not just the list of early reforms, but his whole style of monarchy which impressed both his own people and foreigners. Frederick made it clear that he was uninterested in the medieval and superstitious trappings of monarchy. He described a crown as 'merely a hat which lets the rain in' and he had a modest coronation ceremony.

This was followed by his appearance on the balcony of his palace in Berlin to receive the cheers of the crowds. This sort of behaviour, which today we take for granted from our Royal family in an age of democratic monarchy, was unheard of previously in Prussia.

It was clear too that Frederick was thoroughly enjoying being King. He wrote to one friend 'I must now write to the King of France, compose a solo for the flute, a poem for Voltaire, alter some army regulations and do a thousand other things'. The poem to Voltaire read:

1 My heart on my people dotes,
  This God only will I serve
  Fare ye well then joyous notes
  Verses, flute no time deserve
5 Pleasures all – even Voltaire
  I abjure; duty alone
  I as my sole God enthrone
  Heavy is the crown I wear!

At about the same time Frederick was also writing to Voltaire summing up his current attitude both to his late father and the tasks before him:

1 The ceaseless toil which has fallen to my lot since my father's death leaves me scarcely any time for my natural feelings of grief. Since the loss of my father I have come to believe that I ought to devote myself entirely to my country. In this spirit I have worked
5 to the best of my ability to take the promptest measures for the public good. I at once began by increasing the forces of the state by sixteen battalions, five squadrons of hussars and a squadron of Lifeguards. I have laid the foundations of a new Academy. I have established a new College for trade and industry. I engage
10 painters and sculptors. I am leaving for (East) Prussia to receive homage etc without the useless and frivolous ceremonies imposed by ignorance and superstition, and hallowed by custom.

However, observers who had confidently predicted that he would spend all his time on culture and leave his ministers to run the government were soon disillusioned. Within an hour of becoming King he was warning Prince Leopold of Anhalt-Dessau that he could keep his position as commander of the army, but 'as for authority, I am the only one to exercise authority in this country'. Far from reducing the size of the army, he immediately ordered it to be increased by 10 000 men. His friends from Rheinsburg, looking forward to senior positions and wealth, found they were given only minor appointments and that Frederick no longer had much time for them. The new King kept all his father's old ministers in place, now wore army uniform all the time and confided in nobody. 'If my shirt knew what I was planning I would tear it off'. He promptly separated from his wife and continued to treat her coldly for the rest of their long marriage, even taking it to the point where he refused to let her come and see him when he lay dying in 1786 on the grounds that he was too busy.

  * One of his first wishes was to meet his hero, Voltaire. Their first meeting in 1740 lasted only a few days, but was enough to renew their mutual admiration. Frederick, using the comparisons with famous people from Ancient Rome which were fashionable at the time, described Voltaire as having 'the eloquence of Cicero, the gentleness of Pliny and the wisdom of Agrippa'. Voltaire in return commented that Frederick 'has wit and charm' and then added the cynical afterthought: 'and besides he is a King'. This comment provides a clue to the true nature of their relationship. Certainly they admired each other. From 1736 until Voltaire died they wrote to each other frequently with what seems like insincere flattery. 'Sire' runs one typical phrase from Voltaire, 'you are worthy of adoration. You are, perhaps, the greatest monarch that ever sat on a throne' and again 'under your auspices Berlin will be the Athens of Germany, perhaps of Europe', whilst in return Frederick could write that 'my actions will be the fruit of your teaching'. No doubt this mutual admiration was very satisfying for them both, but it also served a purpose. Frederick, a genuine intellectual himself, was naturally pleased to be treated with such deference by the man Europe recognised as the greatest brain and wit of his age, but he could also see that such a friendship might serve a useful propaganda purpose. In his book *Les Matinées du Roi de Prusse* of 1764 he admitted freely that he used *philosophes* like Voltaire and D'Alembert to help establish his own literary reputation, because he liked being flattered, because he wanted to be famous and because he knew that people respected the judgments of these men.

  In return Voltaire received protection. Frequently in trouble with his own government because of his writings, he knew it would do him no harm to be on friendly relations with the powerful monarch of another state. In addition Voltaire hoped that Frederick might actually put some of his ideas into practice. However, Voltaire made it clear more than once that he did not actually rate Frederick's intellect as highly as he pretended. When Frederick sent him poems to comment on, Voltaire wrote back praising them, whilst confiding to a friend that they were 'more dirty linen to be washed'.

  From 1750–3 Voltaire lived with Frederick in Prussia. Facing problems in France and tempted by generous offers of money, a senior post at court, and Prussia's highest honour, the *Pour le Mérite*, Voltaire spent three years as a permanent dinner guest. At first the two men got on well, but before long they started to quarrel. Voltaire made no secret of his boredom when Frederick told stories of the battles he had fought and won, and he even dared to criticise Maupertuis, Frederick's choice as President of the Prussian Academy. Eventually Voltaire left.

Frederick II

Frederick had him stripped of his post and honour, and even arranged to have him arrested for a time. Voltaire got his revenge by spreading sly stories that Frederick was a homosexual and a sadist. The rift did not last long; both men needed each other too much. The friendly correspondence was resumed, the mutual admiration returned, but they never met each other again. In the final analysis it seems that neither man really liked the other, and that whilst there was genuine respect between them, they both realised the political advantages of being friends with each other. Certainly Frederick benefited from the publicity Voltaire gave him. The fact that we still call him 'The Great' today is due in no small measure to Voltaire, who first suggested the title early in his reign.

Between 1740 and 1763 Frederick's reign was dominated by foreign policy, particularly the War of Austrian Succession and the Seven Years War. Despite these distractions, Frederick's intellectual interests did not diminish. In fact it is astonishing just how much he did achieve, given his other commitments. He particularly enjoyed writing – 'Whenever I have a few moments to spare, I am seized by a desire to write'. He wrote thousands of verses, several epic poems, some major historical works (including a history of his own wars which is still used by historians today), two political testaments, and thousands of essays, memoranda and letters. His collected works total over 100 volumes – and every word of it is in French. Frederick despised his own language and felt it completely lacked the subtlety of French. Today his poetry is not highly regarded, but experts still admire the style of his prose works. He also continued to play the flute well, and composed over 100 works. Some of these are still performed today, and one of them was for 50 years the Spanish national anthem. The quality of his writing and composing suggests that he was the only monarch of the eighteenth century who would still be remembered today even if he had never been a king. He also read widely, again strongly favouring French literature. He had an extensive library and once completed reading and making notes on a 36-volume history of the Church whilst besieging a town in Silesia. However, the library did not have a single book either by a German author or written in German.

There is no doubt that Frederick, although a highly talented author and composer, held very strong prejudices. Not only did he feel that German was a non-literary language, but he totally ignored the German Enlightenment. Although not as well-known as the French version, the German Enlightenment was also flourishing at this time. Writers such as Lessing, Herder, Kant, Winckelmann and Goethe were unread, ignored, or dismissed by the King of Prussia. He made no attempt to encourage German culture in his own universities, whilst only five out of eighteen members of the Prussian Academy were German. Frederick could be similarly dismissive of other areas of culture. Both Haydn and Mozart, two of the most justly famous composers of their age, were casually dismissed as 'degenerate'. His prejudices extended to Shakespeare – 'abominable pieces', and to science, mathematics and astronomy. What is striking about Frederick is that he combined a real intellectual flair with the sort of narrow-minded prejudice for which he had despised his father.

* Not only did he despise German culture, he also despised his own people. Here was one area where he completely differed from the *philosophes* with their stress on humanitarianism and the rights of ordinary people. Frederick had a cynical view of mankind. He was not

interested in the popularity he enjoyed after his wars – 'put a monkey on a camel and you'd get the same response' – and regretted that fate had led him to rule such a primitive people as the Prussians. Towards the end of his reign he complained that he was 'bored of ruling over slaves', but never seems to have questioned whether he or his system of government might be partly to blame for their lack of culture.

One of Frederick's most important monuments is the palace of Sans Souci (meaning 'Without a care' – in French, naturally) built near Potsdam in the years after 1745. Frederick personally supervised its building and decoration, and spent many happy months at this pleasant palace. Here he could recapture some of the enjoyment of Rheinsburg. One can picture Frederick with Voltaire and other exclusive guests enjoying an intellectual discussion over dinner before listening to Frederick playing one of his own compositions on the flute. The atmosphere would have been relaxed, intellectual, light-hearted and witty. This was a strong contrast with Frederick William's idea of a good time, but in one respect at least father and son were the same. Both made their chosen entertainments all male preserves. Frederick's idea that women were incapable of intellectual achievement can be counted as one more prejudice to add to his collection.

In his will Frederick asked to be buried in the grounds of Sans Souci alongside his dogs. This wish nicely sums up both his love of this palace, and his cynical attitude towards rituals such as burial. Inevitably the wish was not granted. His successor, anxious to promote a more serious image for the late King, buried him next to his father at the garrison church at Potsdam with full military honours.

Frederick was able to retain the admiration of the *philosophes* until the end. He was admired even by the German intellectuals whom he despised. In reality he had done little to deserve their admiration. Even his own intellect, although undoubtedly of high calibre, was narrow and prejudiced. Frederick did have the ability to flatter and to make use of the writers and thinkers; they were so pleased to be noticed at all, Frederick's faults could be ignored in their entirety.

3 Education

In common with other Enlightened rulers, Frederick claimed that it was important to encourage the education of his people. To D'Alembert he wrote that 'the more one advances with age, the more one is convinced of the harm done to society by the neglected education of youth'. He was King of a country where hardly any children went to school, and where an earlier decree of his father's setting up some state school was largely ignored.

In practice Frederick's interest in education was spasmodic. It compares unfavourably with the efforts being made in countries such as Russia, Austria and France. His only important decree on education was made in 1763 as part of a series of measures designed to improve the state of the country after the devastation of the Seven Years War. (It is significant that Frederick had done nothing for education in the first 23 years of his reign.) The decree looked impressive on paper. It called for the setting up of a national system of state schools. All children were expected to attend school between the ages of 5 and 13, and there were to be fines for non-attendance. Teachers were to be recruited largely from the ranks of soldiers discharged after the wars. The decree went into detail about how the schools were to be administered, the curriculum, teachers' salaries and the provision of textbooks – free to poorer students. Even a system of schools inspectors was established. In theory Frederick had founded a comprehensive and modern education system, and one which would be applauded by the *philosophes*. Whilst it would be easy today to criticise the narrowness of the curriculum, with its emphasis on loyalty and military skills for the boys and domestic duties for the girls, it must be remembered that this was in line with the thinking then current on educational provision. Rousseau's new ideas on the subject expressed in *Émile* had only been published in the previous year, and did not yet carry any weight in Europe. Most thinkers at this time would have supported the state-centred education favoured by Frederick.

A more serious criticism of these educational reforms is that they were largely ineffective. Very little money was allocated for education – the army continued to swallow up the bulk of the taxes, even in peacetime – and while large numbers of schools seem to have been built, there was a shortage of trained teachers. No state teacher training colleges were established, although some private training colleges were built. The attempt to recruit ex-soldiers as teachers can only be seen as a way of finding useful employment for the troops Frederick no longer needed, since there is no reason to suppose they were any more educated or literate than the children they were supposed to teach. The numbers of schools built varied widely from one province to another. In Cleves hardly any schools functioned, whilst in West Prussia some 750 schools (mostly very small) were in existence in the 1770s. Given a choice between defending his state and educating his people, Frederick, in common with other Enlightened Despots, had no doubt where his priorities lay.

Again in common with his contemporaries, there is doubt whether Frederick, for all his fine words to D'Alembert, actually favoured education for peasant children at all. He wrote that 'It is enough for the people to learn only a little reading and writing . . . they should only receive that which is essential to them, and which is designed to keep them in the villages'. Frederick had no wish for the peasants to start getting ideas above their station.

Frederick was also ambivalent in his attitude towards higher education. One might have expected this most intellectual of eighteenth-century monarchs to have been a keen supporter of Prussia's universities and Academy. However, his attitude was soured by his cynicism towards German culture and people. He did, it is true, revive the Prussian Academy, both its President and most of its members were foreign. His two universities at Halle and Konigsberg were starved of funds and struggled to survive during his reign. One looks in vain for any new institutions of higher education of the type being established in Russia.

Overall there is a strong contrast between Frederick's own education and intellectual attainment and the achievements of Prussian education. Under Frederick, the quality of Prussian education fell below that in many other countries. Outside some limited improvements in primary education, it is debatable whether he achieved any more than his father who had never pretended to be in favour of educating his people.

4 Serfdom

The vast bulk of the people were, of course, peasants. Serfdom in Prussia had never been as oppressive as in Russia or Poland, and in some parts of his scattered country serfdom had died out before Frederick was born. However, there were still large numbders of serfs working on crown lands and the lands of the *Junker* nobles in East Prussia.

Frederick, in common with most of the thinkers of his age, was opposed to serfdom in principle. He called its existence 'abominable', and accurately described his serfs as 'beasts of burden'. In his *Essays on the Forms of Government* he wrote:

1 Serfdom, of all conditions, is the most unhappy, and that at which humanity most revolts. Certainly no man was born to be the slave of his equal.

Throughout her reign Catherine II of Russia had to face the choice between maintaining serfdom (pleasing the nobles and facing peasant revolts), and abolishing it (pleasing the peasants and angering the nobles). It was fortunate for Frederick that he never had to make such a difficult choice. What is striking about Frederick's Prussia is the absence of those serf revolts which were so frequent in Russia. Alan Palmer, in his biography of Frederick, claims this was because the Prussians were by nature 'docile', but this seems far too sweeping a generalisation to explain the apparent lack of resentment towards the institution. Perhaps more helpful in explaining their passivity is the relative lightness of their tax burden. Even during the most expensive years of war, peasants only paid around 40 per cent of their income in taxation – a proportion that we might consider excessive today, but one which was significantly lower than peasants paid in France or Russia, and one which did not increase at all during Frederick's reign. Another factor was the relatively light burden of conscription. Whereas in Russia the conscripted peasant was sent away for 25 years and would probably never be seen by his family again, in Prussia the conscript was usually trained locally under the Canton system introduced by Frederick William, and might well be back on his land, working part-time at least, within two years. Finally, Frederick's system of state granaries ensured that even in years of bumper harvests the peasant got a good price for his produce, whilst in lean years the corn was sold cheaply to prevent starvation. Here we see Frederick at his best, as a paternalistic ruler ensuring that prices remained stable and that his people did not go hungry.

Frederick probably did wish to help relieve the burden of serfdom, but he achieved little in practice. The physical ill-treatment of serfs was illegal and from time to time prosecutions took place. But the fact that such legal action against the nobles was rare might suggest that it was difficult in practice to enforce the law. Some protection was given to peasants in keeping control over their own land by banning the practice of nobles' enclosure of peasants holdings. Nobles were reminded that they were not to work their serfs for more than four days a week. This was as far as Frederick would go. In the *Essays on the Forms of Government* he explained:

1 Whoever should suddenly desire to abolish this abominable administration would entirely overthrow the mode of managing estates and must be obliged to indemnify the nobility for the losses their rents must suffer.

He knew that the abolition of serfdom would anger the nobles and create a social revolution, and this was a risk which he felt was neither necessary nor desirable. His failure to do more to help the serfs suggests that it was not just monarchs with a shaky claim to the throne, like Catherine, who had reason to treat the nobles with respect. The experience of Joseph II of Austria was to show just how dangerous it was to antagonise the nobles. In addition, Frederick had no wish to disrupt a system which provided his army recruits – crucial if Prussia was to survive as a state at all.

His failure to do much to help the serfs of nobles is understandable, given the problems implicit in any reform and the lack of urgency. Less understandable is his failure to end serfdom on crown lands. It seems that for all his enlightened views, Frederick could not conceive of any changes to the social structure of Prussia that he had inherited. It was left to a far weaker King of Prussia, Frederick William III, to free the crown serfs without difficulty in 1798.

5 The Economy

Frederick certainly had a real interest in developing agriculture. He was aware of, and actively promoted the use of, the latest ideas on farming coming from England and Holland. These included crop rotation, selective breeding of animals, the growing of potatoes and turnips – then new crops – and the use of fertilisers. He was particularly interested in developing agriculture in the years after 1763, for he had been worried by the evidence of devastation of his lands during the Seven Years War. He claimed himself that much of Prussia was in as bad a state as it had been during the Thirty Years War (1618–1648) with 6000 homes in one province alone (Silesia) destroyed. Whilst there is no reason to doubt that the Prussian economy had been seriously weakened by the wars, there are also grounds for thinking that Frederick may have exaggerated the extent of the devastation in order to make the recovery programme seem all the more impressive. Nevertheless, there is no doubting the high priority Frederick gave to the restoration of farming. When the wars ended in 1763 he returned to his capital, Berlin. After greeting his wife, whom he had not seen for several years, with the (typically) hurtful comment 'Madam has grown fatter', his first peacetime action was to instruct his officials to draw up lists of food, seed and animals needed in each district. He then spent some 40 million thalers – the equivalent of over two years income from taxes – on distributing free grain, fodder and livestock. The *Junkers* could obtain loans at low rates of interest to develop their lands. There was also an ambitious programme of clearing wastelands and swamps and supporting new villages and tree-planting.

Encouraging immigration to build up Prussia's population was not a new idea. Immigrants were offered the usual inducements of free land and tax exemptions, but Frederick went further than other kings in welcoming all immigrants regardless of their race or religion. He believed that it was not merely necessary, but actually desirable to have a large non-German element in his country. By the end of his reign hundreds of new villages had been established and as much as one fifth of his population were non-Germans. In all, about 300 000 immigrants came to Prussia during his reign.

The result was an impressive growth in both population and agricultural production. 'The real strength of a state' observed Frederick 'consists in the number of its subjects'. By these standards Prussia had done well. Despite wartime population losses, by the end of his reign the number of people in Prussia had doubled to over five million – including of course the Silesians and Poles acquired through conquest. Farming was developing well in a country of poor climate and soil – 'the sand-box of the Holy Roman Empire' – with, for example, the number of farm animals doubling between 1763 and 1786. He had been particularly careful in the development of his two new provinces, Silesia and West Prussia, both of which prospered under efficient Prussian rule.

In farming matters Frederick showed that he was aware of the latest ideas, but this was not the case in industry or trade. At a time when some of the writers were advocating new theories of economics, Frederick stuck to the increasingly old-fashioned theories of mercantalism. He summed up the aims of this theory himself: 'Two things are conducive to the welfare of the country, (1) Bring in money from other countries (2) prevent money leaving the country'. Armed with this over-simple theory, Frederick followed the normal mercantalist economic ideas, encouraging industry, exports and trade, whilst discouraging imports with high duties. New industries were developed, including textiles and porcelain, the mines of Silesia were exploited, and new ministries were set up to supervise them. Canals were built, rivers dredged, ports developed and trading companies started. A state bank was founded along with a state marine insurance company. Exports flourished, and Prussia became one of the most industrialised states in Eastern Europe – not that difficult given the backwardness of most of the area. However, in comparison with other German states, Prussian industrial development was nothing spectacular.

It is not difficult to criticise Frederick's lack of awareness of new economic ideas or his over-regulation of industry, but his policies worked well enough for his purposes. They enabled Prussia to establish herself as a Great Power, maintain an enormous army and give her people a modestly improved standard of living.

* By the standards of most European states, the people of Prussia were taxed lightly, paying less than two thalers a year on average – a figure that hardly altered through Frederick's reign. This represented slightly less than half of the average peasant's income – rather less than peasants in most other countries expected to pay. Frederick's financial policies certainly worked in the sense that his people were not oppressively taxed, he was able to maintain a large army, and he even left his incompetent successor, Frederick William II, a treasury of 50 million thalers. However, these same policies aroused more resentment than anything else Frederick did. Because he was dissatisfied with the income coming in from his own tax-collectors, he replaced them by a group of French tax-farmers who were given control of the *Régie* – the duties on a wide range of consumer goods including alcohol and meat. These tax-farmers were given salaries four times greater than their Prussian counterparts, and were allowed to keep five per cent of what they collected in addition. The result was a massive increase in the duties, a handful of very rich Frenchmen, and considerable resentment from the Prussian people. This episode tells us a little about Frederick's financial policies, and a great deal about what he thought of his own civil servants and his admiration of the French.

Overall, it is hard to find much evidence of enlightenment in

Frederick's economic and financial policies. What he did provide was an efficient and paternalistic attitude towards the economy.

6 Religion

It was in his religious policies that Frederick came closest to the ideals set out by the thinkers of the eighteenth century. He shared with them a strong hostility to religious rituals and superstition and a support for religious toleration. By extending toleration even to non-Christian religions, Frederick can claim to have been the most tolerant ruler in Europe, and this toleration earned the admiration of the *philosophes*.

The motives for Frederick's toleration were mixed. It has been suggested that his harsh upbringing drove out his childhood belief in God and that his generally cynical attitude towards mankind made him look at religion as a way of keeping people quiet. He commented that 'all Religions rest on a system of fable, more or less absurd'. In addition his genuinely held view of the monarch's job as being merely 'The First Servant of the State' led him to argue that it was not his responsibility to interfere with people's religious beliefs. Such an attitude would have shocked monarchs in earlier centuries. They would have argued that, as believers in the Divine Right of Kings, ensuring their subjects followed the true faith was a major, even the most important, of all the tasks God had put them on earth to undertake.

Religious toleration was nothing new in Prussia. Frederick William, although a committed Calvinist, had allowed people of other faiths both to enter and to worship freely in Prussia. Frederick, by continuing this policy, was merely doing what was necessary to ensure a steady flow of immigrants from those countries whose rulers continued to practise persecution. However, from the start of his reign Frederick made it clear that he intended to take his views much further than his father. His refusal to undergo the usual elaborate coronation ceremony on the grounds that it was all ignorance and superstition showed that he was not interested in the mystical religious aspects of monarchy. This did not change as the years went by. He would not sleep in his state bed. He dressed scruffily, chatted to his servants, and strolled in the streets. Press censorship remained light by eighteenth-century standards. Writers and cartoonists were always allowed to poke fun at the King. 'My subjects say what they like. I do what I like' was his comment when someone expressed surprise at the satires on him that were allowed. Not for him the elaborate ceremonial of the French court of Versailles. In many ways this attitude marked a major step forward from the semi-divine image of monarchy of much of Europe.

Frederick practised religious toleration for all Christian groups. In his 1752 *Political Testament* he summarised his attitude:

1 I am the Pope of the Lutherans and Head of the Reformed

Church. All Christian sects are tolerated here. We stop the mouth
of the first man who wants to spark off a civil war. I am neutral
between Geneva and Rome. In this way I diminish religious
5 animosities, and I strive to unite them by showing them that they
are all citizens.

Frederick was not unique in tolerating all Christian groups. Where
he was unique was in extending this toleration to Muslims. This
attitude caused consternation to his officials and delight to the *philosophes*. It was easy for Frederick to take this line since there were, in
fact, no Muslims in Prussia and his offer to build a mosque for them in
Berlin was never taken up. More revealing is Frederick's attitude to the
one group of non-Christians that *did* live in Prussia – the Jews. Here he
showed the same prejudice as other rulers. Jews were the one group not
allowed in as immigrants. Native Jews had to pay special taxes and were
banned from most jobs, including the professions and civil service.
Frederick's attitude towards the Jews shows his real motive for not
doing more for them:

1 As for the Jews, they are poor devils who are not as bad as people
  think. They pay well.

Frederick was prepared to go along with the popular prejudices of
the day when he stood to gain financially. Whilst he shared the same
outlook on religion as the enlightened thinkers, his motives included a
large dose of cynicism and practical politics.

7 The Law and the State

The work of reforming and codifying the Prussian legal system was
started by Frederick when, towards the end of his reign, he appointed
Samuel von Cocceji – actually born into the middle class despite the
noble title – to supervise the work. Cocceji continued until his death in
1755. Others then continued the task and the final sections were not
completed until the 1790s, some years after Frederick's death. Like
many of the reforms ascribed to Frederick, this major achievement had
its roots in the reign of his father. Cocceji seems to have been the only
one of his ministers who was given a free hand, to be trusted, and to
have had the full support of the King.

The law reform was a major achievement – Treasure calls it 'the glory
of his reign' – and it was certainly the most comprehensive codification
of German law in the eighteenth century. Most of Frederick's new legal
structure was to survive until 1900, making it the longest-lasting of his
reforms. As well as giving a common legal system to the scattered
Prussian provinces, the reform provided new protection for the people
of Prussia. There was now equality under the law, guaranteed civil

rights and the right to own property and land. Religious and intellectual freedom were protected. Lawyers and judges had to be trained professionals, and the legal system was made speedier, cheaper and more efficient. It confirmed the various rights and social distinctions enjoyed by the nobles, but, unlike Catherine II's Charter of the Nobility, gave no new rights to them. Overall it gave Prussia a fair legal system, and one in which a poor person might actually win justice against a rich person. It was, Gooch claims, 'a better system then any in Europe, except where constitutional government prevailed, and it formed a bridge between feudalism and the modern democratic state'.

However, although Frederick was genuinely anxious to see justice administered fairly, he also used his own powers in an arbitrary manner. The new system allowed the monarch to dismiss judges at will, and Frederick showed, particularly in his later years, an eagerness to intervene personally in legal cases. In one case he had a priest executed without trial for saying that desertion from the army was a serious, but not a mortal, sin. He threw his Director of Mines into prison because the mines were not producing enough. In the notorious case of the miller Arnold, he repeatedly intervened on Arnold's behalf, and ensured that he won his case against the noble on whose land he lived. Frederick liked to cite this as an example of how even the humblest citizen could obtain justice against a powerful noble by petitioning his monarch. Unfortunately he had chosen poorly, since Arnold was actually in the wrong and the noble was in the right.

Frederick's personal intervention in this case was typical of his whole approach to government. He wanted to retain tight personal control over all aspects of his country. He distrusted and despised his own ministers and civil servants. There were inspections and checks undertaken personally by the King for several months each year. Here too he followed the practice started by his father. He also greatly extended the role of the *Fiscals*, civil servants, often quite junior in rank, who were encouraged to spy on the senior officials. This created an atmosphere of distrust, which suited Frederick completely. He made it clear that he distrusted his civil servants, reminded them that the humblest soldier was more use to him than they were, and ensured that they worked hard for low pay. Yet in reality Frederick's civil service was the envy of Europe. There were fewer of them, they worked harder, but were more honest and achieved more than virtually any other in Europe.

Frederick had a similar attitude towards his ministers. None, apart from Cocceji, was allowed any freedom or initative – 'The orders of the Commander in Chief are to be strictly followed'. So Frederick did the bulk of their tasks himself, working for several hours a day on his papers. Even the smallest decision had to be referred to him. In theory he made no major changes to the system of government established by his father. In practice he increasingly by-passed the General Directory.

This was the central organ of government established by Frederick William, through which the King gave his orders. Fearing that this institution might become too powerful, Frederick created a series of new Ministries and Departments which were answerable directly to him, including the Ministries of Mines and Forests, and the administration of Silesia. Even here the civil servants were constantly reminded of their status – 'You have no right of initiative whatsoever. All matters must be reported to me directly'.

The system worked – after a fashion. Prussia was still a small enough state and the King was sufficiently hardworking for decisions to be made reasonably speedily and fairly. There is no doubt that Frederick was the most industrious king of the eighteenth century, and that he was able to cope with the task of ruling Prussia virtually single-handed. It was a remarkable achievement for one man – but it was to have disastrous consequences. Mirabeau, the astute French observer who was to play an active role in the early stages of the French revolution, visited Prussia just before Frederick died and noted:

1 The mistakes of kings must be included when one reckons the strength of states. The Prussian monarchy is so constituted that it can support no calamity whatsoever, not even the one which is inevitable in the long run – a government without ability . . . One
5 man, even the best of men, cannot do everything . . . If ever a foolish Prince ascends this throne, the giant will collapse and Prussia will fall like Sweden.

The system depended too heavily on the hard work of the monarch. For 70 years Prussian people, civil servants and ministers had been taught to obey orders and not show any initiative. There was of course no question of any assembly or parliament for the people to express their views. Prussia would be paralysed under an ineffective king.

Frederick was well aware that his successor, his nephew Frederick William II, was an amiable fool. Yet he made no attempt to train him to his responsibilities – not even with the cruel methods that his father had used on him. Nor did he consider setting up an alternative system of government that would be able to function under a lazy king. Frederick left his successor 50 million thalers and gloomy predictions that Prussia would collapse without his steady hand. It was as if he had little interest in what happened to his country after he died – or possibly that he wanted his nephew to fail so that his own achievements would not be overshadowed.

8 The Nobles and the Army

The army was at the centre of Prussian life. Even after the wars ended it remained at a huge size to act as a deterrent against Austria. By the end of Frederick's reign it had reached 200000 men, and represented four per cent of the population of Prussia – the same percentage as in Frederick William's time and easily the highest of any state in Europe. The deterrent worked. After 1763, apart from the brief 'Potato War' of 1778, nobody dared take on the feared Prussian army. The majority of taxes continued to flow into the army, and Frederick showed tireless devotion to inspecting his troops and taking them on exercises.

However, the impression of might was misleading. The Prussian army was in fact in serious decline by 1786. Frederick knew it, and did nothing about it. The spectacular battles the army had won in the 1750s had made Frederick complacent about its quality. After the Seven Years War neither the army nor Frederick saw any need to change its tactics or weapons. The French army, shattered by Frederick in 1757, had been reformed and by the 1780s had developed those new weapons and tactics which would prove so useful to Napoleon. Frederick ignored all this. To ease the burden of conscription, he relied increasingly on foreign mercenaries. By 1786 up to half of his soldiers were not Prussian at all. As they were less eager to fight and die for their country, discipline was made even harsher, and the desertion rate became the highest of any army in Europe. Frederick had been obliged to use non-noble officers during his wars, but the bulk of these were sacked after 1763. Only nobles, Frederick felt, had the 'honour' and upbringing to command. As a result he dismissed many of his ablest officers, replacing them with men of high birth but little talent. The trend continued after 1786, until by 1806 less than ten per cent of army officers were not nobles – and nearly all non-noble officers held junior positions.

Frederick saw clear evidence of the decline of the army during the 'Potato War' of 1778 (sometimes called the War of Bavarian Succession) when the soldiers spent their time foraging instead of fighting. Yet he did nothing to reform the army, predicting, correctly, that its huge size and his reputation were all that were needed to deter. What is surprising is that the myth of the mighty Prussian army lasted as long as it did. Not until 1806 did anyone seriously challenge Prussian power – and then Napoleon found that Prussia was the easiest of all his enemies to crush. Obviously Frederick cannot be held responsible for the fact that none of his successors reformed the army in the 20 years after he died. However, he can be criticised for relying too heavily on his own reputation in the years after 1763 and for not reforming the army after 1778 when it was clear how much its quality had slipped.

The fact that Frederick actively favoured the use of nobles in the Prussian army is only one example of the way in which the nobility was quietly restoring its power in Prussia. In theory the nobles had as few rights as anyone else. They had no Estates to represent their views, and they too took orders from the King. In reality Frederick increasingly relied on them as the one reliable and loyal group in Prussia. They came to dominate the higher ranks of the army, the civil service and the judiciary. The reforms in agriculture made them increasingly prosperous, and they were allowed to form local groups which, whilst in theory restricted to discussing farming problems, were actually encouraged to discuss anything of concern to them and to advise the King of their concerns. Under Frederick they enjoyed an important, but clearly subordinate, role. Under Frederick's weak successors they inevitably took more power and began that dominance of Prussian society that was to be such a feature of Prussia, and then Germany, until 1945. Professor Kraus at Konigsberg University summed up the state of Prussia a few years after Frederick's death:

1 The Prussian state, far from being an unlimited monarchy, is but a thinly veiled aristocracy. This aristocracy rules the country in thinly disguised form as a bureaucracy.

9 Conclusion

The 1770s were perhaps Frederick's finest years, with his justifiably high reputation as a military genius and his country recognised as a Great Power, well on the way to recovery after the wars. It was a time when civil servants, for all his nagging, were 'proud to work for the King of Prussia', known for his fairness and hard work. There were no opinion polls to tell us what his people thought of him, but the affectionate (if disrespectful) nickname – 'Der Alte Fritz' ('Old Fred') and the lack of peasant revolts suggest that he was respected if not loved. However, during the 1780s his increasing interference in justice, his worsening temper and perhaps simply boredom with a ruler who had exercised paternal control for over 40 years meant his people came to dislike him. He was aware that he had outlived his times and was unable to change. When he did die in 1786 Mirabeau recorded that 'there was no grief . . . they were tired of him'.

Frederick saw himself as 'The First Servant of the State'. This phrase, which he was fond of using, was not in fact his – it had been used for centuries, although it is arguable that Frederick was the first to take it seriously. In his *Essays on the Forms of Government* of 1771 he summed up both his feelings about the role of the King, and his awareness of its limitations:

1 The ruler must often remind himself that he is a man like the least of his subjects – the first judge, the first general, the first financier, the first minister. He is only the first servant of the state, obliged to act with wisdom and disinterestedness, as if at
5 any moment he had to render an account of his administration to his citizens. He is the head of a family and must be the last refuge of the unhappy, a father to orphans, the succour of widows,

caring for the meannest unfortunate. With the best will in the
world, he can make mistakes; he can be misinformed; his orders
10 may not be executed; injustices may never reach his ear; officials
may be too severe. In a word, he cannot be everywhere.
Therefore, in governing, as in everything else, we must be
content with what is least defective.

This is a revealing passage. In it he stresses the role of the King as
servant and worker, working for the state rather than ruling it. His
famous 'First Servant' phrase can be contrasted with the (alleged)
remark of Louis XIV of France, made about 100 years previously: 'I am
the State' (*L'État c'est moi*). The three words which Frederick added to
Louis' equally famous statement of how he perceived the role of King,
indicate the difference between Divine Right monarchy and Enlightened Despotism.

Frederick certainly did work tirelessly for the state. In the passage
above he is honest about the limits to the power of even the most
absolute ruler such as himself. But although he claimed that a ruler
must act *as if* he might have to render an account to his people,
Frederick never actually intended to make himself accountable to
anybody. Servant, Frederick might be; but he was a most unusual
servant in that the servant gave himself his own orders.

How enlightened was he? Not very much, it seems, when comparing
his ideas and achievements with the fashionable theories. The *philosophes* had faith in humanity; Frederick despised his people. They
believed in free trade, but he practised mercantalism; they believed that
education would lead to the perfectability of Man; he thought people
were stupid and gave little support to education. In only a few areas did
their ideas match – the admiration for French culture, the support for
religious toleration, and the creation of a fair and equal legal system.

On balance Frederick, like so many of the Enlightened Despots,
picked and chose those of the fashionable theories that suited him and
which helped him to run his country more efficiently; where they did
not, he ignored them. Basically he had far more in common with his
father and his father's style of ruling than with the enlightened
thinkers. An old-fashioned King of Prussia with traditional aims and
values, he was intelligent enough to see the benefits of posing as an
enlightened King and was flattered by the attention he received from
men like Voltaire.

* Frederick's influence on the later history of Prussia was immense,
and it is arguable that the myth surrounding him eventually came to
outweigh his real achievements. In the years after Prussia's collapse in
1806 historians offered a balanced judgment on him, admiring his
achievements but also pointing out his responsibility for the disaster of
1806. In the 1860s, when Bismarck unified Germany, historians
portrayed Frederick as a pioneer of German unification. Ranke and

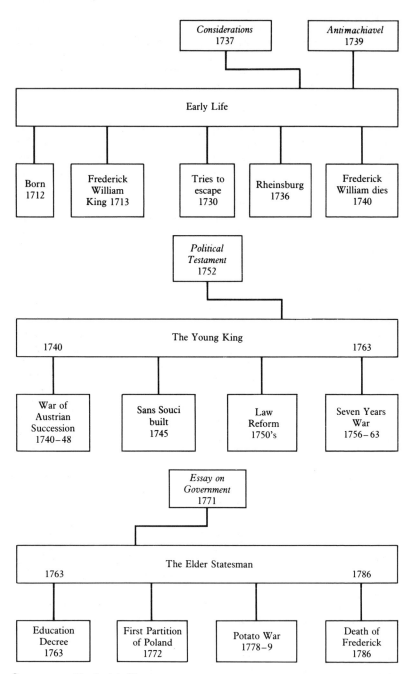

Summary – Frederick II

Treitschke helped create the myth of Frederick as a German nationalist who started the work of expelling the multi-national Austrian Empire from the *Reich*. His foreign policy achievements and the pre-eminent position he gave to the army were praised, whilst his domestic achievements and his love of French culture were played down. Koser, another nationalist historian, summed him up as 'A great King who was also a great man'.

The collapse of the German Empire and the abdication of Kaiser William II, the descendant of Frederick II, did not end the glorification of Frederick. Meinecke stressed that Frederick could best be explained by understanding the conflict between the enlightened ideas which moulded his character and the practical politics which guided his actions. Historians in the Nazi period did not hesitate to portray Frederick as a prototype follower of Hitler. The fall of Nazi Germany has led German historians again to look for a more balanced judgment, although there is still reluctance to look beneath his successes. The 200th anniversary of his death in 1986 led to several books in which both East and West German historians claimed Frederick as a founder of their states.

German leaders from Bismarck to Hitler identified themselves strongly with Frederick. His tomb became a national shrine for important events. This reached its climax with Hitler's hero-worshipping of Frederick, to the extent of closely identifying his situation in 1945 with that of Frederick in 1759. Later nationalists, whether rulers or historians, ignored his admiration for the French and his refusal to speak or write in German. They forgot his religious toleration and his wish to encourage non-German immigration. They admired his vices and ignored his virtues. Frederick, if he had known how his ideas and achievements would be misused by later rulers, would no doubt have felt that it only proved how gullible people are.

Making notes on 'Frederick the Great'

This chapter sets out to analyse to what extent Frederick's domestic policy was 'enlightened', rather than trying to cover all the main events of his reign. Your notes should concentrate on (i) his aims and (ii) his achievements, as well as on (iii) a consideration of how 'enlightened' he was.

The following headings would provide a suitable framework for the detailed notes that you are likely to require on this topic.

1   The New King
1.1. Frederick William's achievements
1.2. Frederick's upbringing and its effects on him
1.3. Early Writings

(In sections 3–8 below look at Frederick's aims, what he achieved, and how 'enlightened' he was.)

Answering essay questions on 'Frederick the Great'

Many essays on Frederick II concentrate on his spectacular foreign policy, which is covered in detail in the companion volume *Habsburgs and Hohenzollerns*. Questions on his domestic policy usually cover one or more of the following aspects:

a) Whether his policies were enlightened
b) The impact of his policies on Prussia
c) The aims of his domestic policy
d) A comparison of Prussia in 1740 and 1786.

Essays on this subject will either ask a direct question on one aspect of Frederick's policies, or offer a quotation for discussion. The first type of question is usually thought to be easier by most students, but this is not, in fact, always the case. Consider this question:

1. 'Is it possible to defend the record of Frederick the Great on the question of domestic reform?'

Of which type of essay listed above is this an example?

A straightforward approach to this question would be to go through the main features of Frederick's domestic policy, discussing in each case what criticisms have been made and whether or not they are justified. However, there is a danger that such an essay might end up being dominated by narrative. A better approach would be to focus on the assumption implicit in the essay title – that Frederick's domestic policy needs defending. Start by listing all the major criticisms that can be made of his domestic policies – and remember to extend this list to include the impact of his policies on the later history of Prussia. You should be able to find at least six major criticisms. Next, for each criticism, look for evidence to support the criticism, selected from any aspects of his domestic policy, and the defence that both Frederick and historians have offered. With this approach you are more likely to produce a wide-ranging essay which is not limited to the actual events of Frederick's reign.

'Challenging statement' essays need a slightly different approach. Look at this example:

> 2. '"The Enlightenment enlightened Frederick, but brought no benefit to his subjects." Discuss.'

The first task whenever you are faced with a 'challenging statement' question is to identify the aspects of the topic in which the examiner is interested. There are two statements here, and you will have to discuss both of them. What are the two statements? In your introduction to a challenging statement essay like this, it is important that you not only introduce the topic of Frederick II in general, but also make it clear that you understand what the quotation is asking, and explain the two questions you will be answering.

One acceptable approach is to treat these as two separate short essays and spend about 20 minutes answering each question, bringing the two halves together at the end. Assume that you are going to adopt this approach and make a list of four paragraph headings for each of the two questions, identifying the examples you would use to support the theme of each paragraph.

However, it would probably be better to treat the quotation as a single statement. This time create an essay plan that covers Frederick's domestic policy, and addresses both aspects of the question within each paragraph. How does it differ from your first plan? Which plan do you think you would find easier to write out as a full essay? Why?

Both approaches will require you to have a concluding paragraph in which you return to the original quotation and offer a clear answer to the two questions you were originally posed. What answers will you give? It is also often a good idea in the conclusion to broaden the essay out and *briefly* to raise other issues not directly asked by the examiner. This will demonstrate the breadth of your knowledge, and your awareness that there is far more to Frederick II than is covered by the relatively narrow question posed here. In this case, for instance, you might wish to balance the criticisms you have made of his domestic achievements with some comment on his military successes and/or his popularity amongst his people.

Source-based questions on 'Frederick the Great'

1 Frederick's attitude towards monarchy

Read the extracts from *Antimachiavel* on page 33, the poem on page 35 and the letter to Voltaire on page 35. Answer the following questions:

a) Explain what is meant by 'Preventative wars' (page 33 line 4), 'This God' (page 35 line 2) and 'The forces of the state' (page 35 line 6). (3 marks)

b) What, according to these sources, is the job of a king? (3 marks)

c) With which parts of these extracts would the *philosophes* have agreed, and with which parts would they have disagreed?
(5 marks)

d) Frederick William died before any of these were published. What might he have thought of them? Give reasons for your answer. (3 marks)

e) In the light of Frederick's later career, which of these sources probably best represents Frederick's real views? Explain your answer. (6 marks)

2 The theory and practice of reform

Read the extracts from *Essays on the Form of Government* on pages 41 and 42, the *Political Testament* on pages 45–6 and the source on page 46. Answer the following questions:

a) What is meant by 'I am the Pope of the Lutherans' (page 45 line 1) and 'neutral between Geneva and Rome' (page 46 lines 3–4)? (4 marks)

b) How did Frederick explain (i) his opposition to serfdom, and (ii) why he was unable to abolish it? (2 marks)

c) Comment on Frederick's justification for his failure to abolish serfdom. (4 marks)

d) What do the extracts on pages 45 and 46 suggest were his real reasons for encouraging religious toleration? (4 marks)

e) What evidence do these extracts offer to support the argument that Frederick was in practice uninterested in real enlightened reform? (6 marks)

3 Assessing Frederick II

Read Mirabeau's comments on page 48, Professor Kraus's views on page 50 and Frederick's comments on pages 50–1. Answer the following questions:

a) What is meant by 'unlimited monarchy' (page 50 line 1), 'thinly veiled aristocracy' (page 50 line 2) and 'furst servant of the state' (page 50 lines 3–4)? (6 marks)

b) What criticisms do Kraus and Mirabeau make of the Prussian system of government? What can be deduced about their own attitudes and values from the criticisms they make?   (4 marks)

c) How does Frederick answer these criticisms in his essay?

(4 marks)

d) Comment on the view that the later history of Prussia proved Kraus and Mirabeau to be right and Frederick wrong. (6 marks)

CHAPTER 4

Catherine the Great

1 Coming to Power

The brilliance of Catherine II of Russia's court, the beauty of the palaces she built, her success in war after war, and her colourful love-life have all given her an image of triumph and achievement matched by few other rulers in eighteenth-century Europe. On the face of it her flattering title – 'The Great' – first bestowed on her by the Assembly she summoned in 1767, seems fully justified by her achievements. In reality, her achievements were largely based on the work of her less glamorous predecessors, and in many instances fell short of the enlightened ideals that she herself proclaimed.

For much of the seventeenth century Russia had been a country of no importance in European affairs. There had been little contact with the western European powers, few of which felt it necessary to keep ambassadors in Moscow. But during the reign of Peter the Great (1689–1725) the situation had changed dramatically. Russia had conquered considerable land from Sweden, enabling Peter to establish his 'Window to the West' which he saw as vital if Russia was to establish herself as a Great Power. However, Peter had less success with his domestic policies, despite being an energetic, not to say ruthless, ruler. The economy had remained backward by western standards. Most of the people were serfs, tied to the land and forced to work for their lord without pay. Serfdom was a relatively new institution in Russia, only becoming widespread in the sixteenth century. Peter had extended it because it enabled him to tap Russia's resources more effectively. Serfs provided the conscripts for his 100 000 strong army which, more by weight of numbers than superior generalship, had enabled him to defeat Charles XII of Sweden. Serfs paid a poll tax which enabled Peter to finance his long wars, and which remained the main source of income for Russian Tsars until the nineteenth century. Serfs were also conscripted to build St Petersburg (now Leningrad), Peter's fine new capital city built on land captured from the Swedes on the Baltic coast facing western Europe. Thousands died building his city on unsuitable marshland.

* Peter left a mixed legacy to his successors. Russia had emerged as a Great Power, but with serious social and administrative problems unsolved. Peter had no clear system of government, expecting simply to give orders and for others to carry them out. He left a regime which was understaffed and inefficient and one in which even minor decisions had to be referred to the Tsar. His death was followed by years of chaos. Between 1725 and 1762 there were no fewer than seven Tsars. Most of them were incompetent. Four of them were women – then regarded by

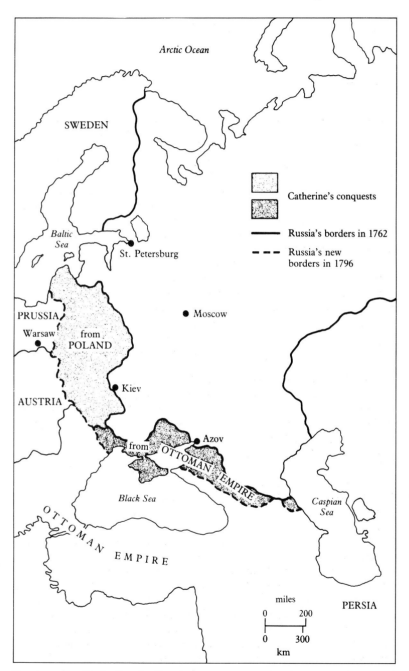

Russia under Catherine the Great

most Russians as an impossible disadvantage for a ruler. There were several *coups d'état* by the army to make and unmake rulers. It seemed that Peter's hard work was going to be undone. Russia became an object for ridicule in western countries. No wonder that when Catherine II came to the throne after yet another *coup* which involved the casual murder of the previous Tsar, her husband Peter III, many foreign observers doubted whether she would last much longer than her unlamented husband.

Certainly, on the face of it, Catherine had few credentials to claim to be the rightful ruler of Russia. She did not have a drop of Romanov blood in her. In fact, she was not even Russian. She had been born in 1729 as Sophie of Anhalt-Zerbst, the daughter of the ruler of one of the smallest and least important of the hundreds of little states which made up the Holy Roman Empire. As a teenage girl she had impressed Frederick II of Prussia with her intelligence and energy – no mean achievement since Frederick was not usually impressed by any woman. It was Frederick who had suggested Sophie as a possible bride for Peter, the nephew and heir to the then Russian Tsarina, Elizabeth (1741–62). In 1744 Sophie undertook the long journey to Russia to marry Peter. The marriage was not a success. Peter treated his wife with contempt. It is uncertain whether he, or Saltykov, the first of Catherine's many lovers, was the father of Catherine's son, Paul.

* Peter III became Tsar in 1762 on the death of Elizabeth, but his reign only lasted a few months. In that time he managed to alienate every section of Russian society. His eccentricities, such as playing for hours with his huge army of toy soldiers, led people to question his sanity. As a Lutheran he made no secret of his contempt for the Eastern Orthodox Church. This was not calculated to endear him to the devout Russian people. He showed his feelings by talking and laughing through Church services, and in a more practical way by seizing the Church's lands. Above all, his astonishing decisions in foreign policy angered the army officers. He ended the Seven Years War against Frederick the Great – a ruler he greatly admired as a real life hero who won battles with real men which he could only win with toy soldiers. He then ordered the Russian army to join forces with Frederick, and finally decided to go to war with Denmark on a trivial pretext.

The result was a plot to overthrow him led by two army officers, the Orlov brothers. The *coup* was easy and virtually bloodless. Peter was murdered, although the official explanation was that he had died of a sudden stomach ache. The throne was offered to his wife, who had now taken the more Russian-sounding name of Catherine. The fact that Gregory Orlov was Catherine's current lover has raised questions about Catherine's involvement in the plot. Although there can never be final proof, it is extremely likely that Catherine organised and led the *coup* herself.

* It is easy to assume that the years 1725–62 were totally wasted years for Russia, whilst a series of extravagant and incompetent Tsars and Tsarinas plotted and intrigued, built palaces, imprisoned their rivals, and plunged their country deeper into debt. In fact, this would be a considerable over-simplification. It is true that no progress was made in many areas, but neither had Russia fallen into decline. This was demonstrated most clearly during the Seven Years War (1756–63). Tsarina Elizabeth joined the coalition of powers fighting Frederick II. The Russian army proved to be the only one capable of defeating the Prussians, and by the time Elizabeth died in 1762, Russian armies had overrun East Prussia and were fighting successfully in Germany – an achievement that was not to be repeated for another 50 years. The other Great Powers of Europe enjoyed no such success during the war. Prussia and Austria fought each other to exhaustion, whilst France was so heavily defeated that she started on the slippery slope to bankruptcy and revolution. In 1762 only Britain, with its extensive colonial conquests could rival Russia as the most powerful single state in Europe.

At home progress was also being made. Important changes were instituted by Elizabeth, and Russia's first university was established. She also took the first steps to modernise the legal system with a reform of the criminal law. It was during her reign that western culture first became fashionable in Russia and trade was encouraged by the abolition of internal customs duties. There was even talk – but only talk – of doing something to ease the plight of the serfs. Finally, it was Elizabeth with her 21-year unchallenged reign who brought Russia a period of stability and autocratic rule. Before her reign Russia had been drifting towards the sort of anarchy found in Poland with all-powerful nobles and puppet kings. After her reign, even the maligned Peter III who succeeded her had introduced a few reforms alongside his blunders. He abolished the secret police, cut taxes on the peasants and, in a major concession to the nobles, abolished State Service. This was the compulsory work in either government or armed forces which Peter the Great had imposed on all nobles. It was much resented by the nobles and had already been reduced in scope by the Empress Anna in the 1730s.

Being Peter the Great's daughter had enabled Elizabeth to overcome the traditional Russian opposition to women rulers. Catherine enjoyed no such advantage of birth. Although Russians of importance were pleased to be rid of the apparently insane Peter III, the new ruler had no legal claim to the throne, which should have gone to Peter's son Paul on his father's death. Catherine could therefore only expect to retain the throne as long as she was able to demonstrate that she was a successful ruler. Otherwise there would always be the danger that the army, which had put her on the throne so easily, might remove her just as casually. Certainly this was something of which Catherine was particularly aware during her first few years. It is even possible to argue that everything she did as Empress was motivated by her desire to retain the throne.

2 *Zemstvo* and *Nakaz*

Catherine was the first Russian ruler who had been given an enlightened education. Whilst a child in Germany she had read with enthusiasm the writings of Voltaire, Montesquieu, Locke and others. She found reading a useful way to pass the time during the dead years between 1744 and 1762 when she was bored and lonely in Russia, with a husband who showed no interest in her and an Empress (Elizabeth) who criticised her for failing to produce an heir.

When she became Empress she continued to read widely. She built up a large library in her palace and claimed that she always kept a book in her pocket to read if she had a few moments free during the day. There is no reason to think that this was untrue. She was a genuinely intellectual and widely-read monarch, proabably the most highly educated ruler Imperial Russia ever had. The question was: would she attempt to put into practice some of the modern ideas about which she had read, or would she continue to govern Russia in the traditional manner?

* Early in her reign, in December 1766, Catherine announced that she wanted delegates to come to Moscow to explain the needs and problems of their communities, and to take part in the preparation of a new code of laws. That Catherine felt the laws needed modernising was no great surprise. Russian law was still based on the old code of 1649. Ever since Peter I's time there had been committees and commissions which had considered modernisation of the legal system, but nothing had been done. The task was too great, and the rulers had other priorities. Law reform seemed unimportant to rulers whose major interest was foreign conquest. Catherine's proposal was far more radical than setting up another small committee.

A large assembly, or *Zemstvo*, representing all groups in Russia was to be elected. The deputies would take part in preparing the new laws themselves. The decision to call together such an assembly was without precedent in Russian history. Commissions had been called once or twice before – although none for over 100 years – but never to discuss the laws of the country. It is significant, too, that no future ruler of Russia was to repeat this experiment until Nicholas II was forced by revolution to allow an assembly to be elected in 1906.

Historians have questions Catherine's motives in calling this assembly. It has been suggested that she wished to become better informed about the opinions and ideas of the Russian people; to legitimise her rule with the 'consent' of the people; to provide a safety valve for discontent; and to put into practice a belief in a partnership between the ruler and her people. Catherine herself never explained her motives, so the relative merits of these arguments are difficult to assess. It is clear that she was well aware of the insecurity of her position amongst the nobles. Some felt that her baby son, Paul, should be Tsar with Catherine merely the Regent; a few were opposed to her for condoning the murder of her husband. Certainly there was jealousy and fear – unfounded as it turned out – that the Orlov brothers were the real rulers of Russia. Rumours that she was thinking of reducing the number of serfs by ordering that they must be freed whenever the land they worked on was sold, was another cause for concern to the nobles.

An indication of the weakness of Catherine's position was the way she only just managed to counter the plan by Nikita Panin, the head of the College of Foreign Affairs, to limit her power with an Imperial Council. He suggested a Council of up to eight members, including four senior ministers. All important laws and orders would require the Council's approval. Panin argued that such a Council would make the government more efficient and prevent in future both the mad decrees of a Peter III and the excessive influence of favourites as had happened under Anna and Elizabeth.

Catherine may well have hoped that the *Zemstvo* would endorse and legitimise her claim to the throne. This would ensure no repetition of plans to end absolute monarchy. There is no doubt that she also had other, more enlightened motives for calling an assembly. She hoped to show the rest of Europe that Russia was no longer the 'Despotism tempered with assassination' of old. Still inexperienced in running a government, she accepted the idea put forward by the writers that government involved consultation and partnership, and that the best laws were those which were made with the consent of the governed. Certainly the decision to call an assembly, which was apparently made against the wishes of some of her advisers, shows boldness and self-confidence for a newly installed ruler. It was in many ways a leap in the dark, for there was no certainty that she would be able to control the debates and decisions. There was every reason to think that Catherine was about to adopt a radically new system of government for Russia.

* When the *Zemstvo* gathered in 1767 it comprised 205 nobles, 167 townspeople, 29 free peasants, 44 Cossacks, 54 from the minority races, plus 29 members representing the government. There were no representatives for the serfs, who made up about 90 per cent of the population. Clearly the assembly was never intended to be a parliament representing all the people in Russia. It is possible that the relatively large number of townspeople elected – large when compared to their numbers and social standing in Russia at this time – represented an attempt by Catherine to have as many potential supporters of her ideas as possible in her assembly.

The fact that delegates were elected was not significant. It was merely a matter of selecting a suitable volunteer from the relevant group in a province. There were no election campaigns, and no secret ballots. It was always intended as a consultative assembly, and there was no question of the *Zemstvo* framing its own new laws. The delegates were there to look at Catherine's proposed laws and to discuss them. In short they were not to act as a check to Catherine's autocratic power. Nevertheless it was a dramatic change for Russia as no previous Tsar had thought it necessary to consult an assembly before making his own laws. The infrequent assemblies and commissions of the past had each been called for one specific and limited purpose. The most recent one, the *Zemsky Sobor* of 1613 had been called to choose a new Tsar after a 30-year civil war.

* Catherine had not finished surprising her people. In the same decree which summoned the *Zemstvo*, she announced that she would be providing her own suggestions on how Russia should be ruled. This was the famous *Nakaz*. The word means 'Instructions', which may be indicative of how Catherine wanted her ideas to be treated. The *Nakaz* was issued in stages. The most important sections were published in 1767, in time for the delegates to read and digest before they started work in the assembly. Nobody knows exactly why Catherine decided to produce this document, or whether she had always intended the *Nakaz* to be discussed by an assembly. She later wrote that:

1 For eighteen months I consulted no one, but was guided solely by my heart and reason.

This is not quite true, as we know that she had shown parts of it in advance to some of her advisers, and that some of them had expressed grave concern at what they read.

The *Nakaz* was not, as is sometimes suggested, a list of laws which she wanted passed. Rather it showed her ideas of what principles should form the basis of laws in Russia. It was in fact a summary of much that was fashionable amongst enlightened thinkers at the time. Catherine never claimed that it was original work. Of the 526 Articles in the *Nakaz*, each of which was a sentence or a paragraph, 294 were based on Montesquieu's *Esprit des Lois*, and a further 108 came from Beccaria's *Crime and Punishment*. Others came from the *Encyclopédie*. In fact very few were thought of by Catherine herself, and some of those were taken virtually word for word from other books. But to criticise her for merely re-writing other people's work misses the point. She wrote the *Nakaz* not to become famous as a writer but to make it possible to put the ideas into practice. Had she actually done so, Russia would have been the first country in Europe to be run on the lines suggested by the enlightened writers.

* The *Nakaz* caused a sensation. Voltaire was deeply impressed and delighted that the ideas of the Enlightenment were about to be put into practice in Russia. He told Catherine that the *Nakaz* was:

1 the most beautiful monument of the century. It will bring you
more glory than ten battles because it is conceived by your own
genius and written by your own fair little hand.

This was typical of the mutually flattering letters Catherine and Voltaire
exchanged at this time. In another, written in December 1767, Voltaire
wrote:

1 Madame, if your Imperial majesty will forgive me, you are surely
the brightest star of the North, and there was never one as
beneficient as you. Others would have let Diderot die of hunger.
He was persecuted in his own country, and you came and sought
5 him out. You go in search of merit, madam, and find it. Your
noble efforts to establish freedom of conscience in Poland are a
blessing to the human race. In the meantime, madam, please
allow me to publish what you were kind enough to write to me
about toleration. Your writings are a monument to your fame.
10 There are three of us, Diderot, D'Alembert and myself, who raise
altars to you. Madam, I fall at your majesty's feet, not merely
with profound respect, but in idolatry.

From the priest of your temple.

Catherine was delighted to have such high praise from so famous a
writer. Voltaire continued to serve the Empress well for the rest of his
life. He never visited Russia, but wrote in glowing terms about her
achievements for the next eleven years. It is largely thanks to his efforts
that her flattering nickname, 'The Great', is still used to describe her
today. The French government of Louis XV was so appalled at the
seditious nature of the book's ideas that it banned the *Nakaz*. Officially
Catherine was shocked by this action; in reality she was probably
delighted, because it confirmed her reputation as an enlightened ruler
with other *philosophes*.
   * What was in this document that so delighted the *philosophes* and so
angered the French government? The following are typical of its list of
526 statements of principle:

1.   The Christian Law teaches us to do Mutual Good to one
another.
6.   Russia is a European State.
9.   The Sovereign is absolute; for there is no other authority but
that which centres in his single Person, that can act with a Vigour
proportionate to the extent of such a vast Dominion.
34.   The Equality of Citizens consists in this: that they should all
be subject to the same Laws.
94.   It is unjust to punish a Thief in the same Manner as another

who commits Murder. Everyone sees clearly that some Difference ought to be made in their Punishment.

123.   The Usage of Torture is contrary to the Dictates of Nature and Reason; even Mankind cries out against it and demands loudly the total Abolition of it.

240.   It is better to prevent crimes than to punish them.

241.   To prevent crimes is the intention of every good Legislation.

248.   The most sure; but at the same time the most difficult Expedient to mend the Morals of the people is a perfect System of Education.

353.   Every parent should refrain in the presence of his children not only from Actions but even Words that tend to Injustice and Violence; as for instance, Quarrelling, Swearing, Fighting and Cruelty; and not to allow those who are about his children to set them bad examples.

515.   It is better for the Sovereign to encourage and for the Laws to threaten.

522.   Nothing now remains for the Commission to do, but to compare every Part of the Laws with the Rules of these Instructions.

Some historians have suggested that the whole document was hypocritical, designed only to impress the *philosophes* in western Europe. The fact that very few of the high ideals were ever put into practice is evidence to support this. Torture was indeed abolished (as it already had been once before by Elizabeth), but no equality under the Law was ever achieved – on the contrary, the later Charter of the Nobility (see page 72) gave nobles and peasants quite distinct and notably different systems of laws and punishments. The way in which the statements were formulated can also be criticised. The articles are full of fine principles, but very little is said about how these ideals might be put into practice. Many of them end up being little more than pious platitudes.

On the key issue of serfdom, the *Nakaz* was vague. Article 253 stated that serfdom ought to be rare, but Article 260 cautiously warned that it would be dangerous to free all the serfs at once. These articles suggest that Catherine felt that the reduction of serfdom should be only a long-term aim. If she was serious about this, the debates in the *Zemstvo* must have made her realise just how difficult such a reform would be. None of the delegates favoured the abolition of serfdom; on the contrary, the townspeople were pressing for the right to own serfs to be extended to them. Since no serfs were elected as delegates, it is not surprising that the views of the people most affected by serfdom were not put forward. Catherine might have invited serfs to the assembly and then used their views as a way of putting pressure on the nobles to reduce serfdom. The fact that she did not is a strong indication that she never intended the *Zemstvo* to initiate any social reform which might have endangered her own position. Catherine may have genuinely wanted improvements to the laws, and may have sincerely wanted to be a consultative ruler, but she had no intention of doing anything that might weaken her own authority. She, unlike some historians, was well aware of the limits to her power.

This is confirmed by the articles on government. Montesquieu's *Esprit des Lois* argued strongly in favour of a limited monarchy, but

Catherine II

Catherine, whilst taking up many of his other ideas, rejected limited monarchy in favour of absolute monarchy as shown in Article 9. Her defence of absolute monarchy as being the only efficient system of government in a large country like Russia, was reasonable. It would have been supported by most of the *philosophes*, who agreed with absolute monarchy. Clearly Catherine was not an uncritical copier of other people's theories; she selected those which she felt were useful and relevant to Russia, but rejected those which might in any way undermine her power. Where she could be enlightened without losing authority, she supported reform; but where enlightenment clashed with despotism, the latter was more important to her.

* The *Zemstvo* met over 200 times between 1767 and 1768. After prolonged debate, the deputies decided to offer Catherine the title 'The Great' for summoning them. However, they were unable to agree on even one law. There were various reasons for this. As might be expected, the different social groups disagreed strongly with one another. The delegates' lack of experience showed in their long debates over trivial issues. In 1768 the outbreak of war with Turkey gave Catherine the excuse to 'temporarily' suspend the meetings of the assembly. It was never reconvened. Presumably Catherine felt that it had served its purpose. It had confirmed that autocracy was the only realistic way to rule Russia, and had given her some indications of the wishes of her people.

The English Ambassador at the time thought the whole exercise was a propaganda ploy to give Catherine an enlightened image abroad and to confirm her power at home. Having achieved its purpose, Catherine got rid of it. This cynical view of Catherine's motives is supported by some historians today. A less machiavellian interpretation is that Catherine was a genuinely enlightened ruler who honestly had high hopes for reform, but who came to realise from the debates in the assembly just how disunited Russia was, how reluctant the nobles were to change, and that what was fine on paper would not work in practice in Russia. She might continue to hope for some reforms, but these would have to come from herself. Nor had the assembly been a complete failure. She had become far better informed about the state of Russia and the views of the different groups (always excepting the serfs) through the statements the delegates brought with them. these can be compared with the *Cahiers* brought by the French delegates to the Estates-General of 1789. The difference is that Louis XVI was never able to make use of his statements, but Catherine had plenty of time to use hers. In addition, much of the work of the sub-committees did lead to new laws in future years, and in particular the great reform of local government of 1775 can be traced back to the work of the assembly in 1767–8. Although the assembly had not passed any laws, the ground-work had been laid, thanks to the sub-committes set up, for later reforms. It was a disappointing result, but not as total a failure as appeared at first sight.

3 Serfdom

One of the most damning indictments of Catherine's claim to be enlightened is her total failure to help the serfs. She came from a country where serfdom was unknown and she was, in theory, totally opposed to it. As well as the hints she dropped in the *Nakaz*, she openly criticised it in letters to her friends. She wrote that 'It is insupportable and cruel and contrary to the Christian religion'. She not only objected to serfdom on moral grounds, but was also aware that it was bad for the Russian economy. When the Free Economic Society was founded in 1765, she encouraged it to launch an essay competition on serfdom; the prize-winner advocated the gradual abolition of serfdom, incentives for increased production by the peasants, and argued along classic physiocratic lines that the peasant, rather than the noble, was the foundation of Russia's wealth. The winner of the second prize put the other point of view; serfdom was wrong because it was immoral for one person to 'own' another. None of the 160 essays entered in the competition favoured the retention of serfdom. This figure might suggest that a significant number of educated Russians were against serfdom. Unforunately only seven of the essays were submitted by Russians. The rest were written by foreigners.

Catherine, who personally authorised the publication of the winning essays, was therefore well aware of the economic arguments against serfdom as being an inefficient means of producing Russia's wealth. But she also knew that few Russian nobles would support her in any move to free the serfs. She could not help but be aware of the degrading effects of serfdom on the peasants and of the corrupting influence it had on the landowners who could do as they wished with their peasants. No system which allowed elderly, grey-bearded men to be flogged for not working hard enough and young girls to be offered for sale in markets could be justified by a supporter of the Enlightenment. She summed up neatly the evils of serfdom when someone criticised the peasants for being so dirty. She replied 'How can you expect them to take care of their bodies which do not belong to them?'

It is therefore surprising that Catherine, who was so opposed to serfdom in theory, not only allowed it to continue but actually extended it. Serfdom was introduced into the Ukraine, the last populous area of Russia with significant numbers of free peasants. Laws were passed allowing nobles to punish serfs in any way they wished, other than by torture or death – although in practice nobles who killed their own peasants were rarely prosecuted. Those who were found guilty were given ludicrously light sentences. One female owner was sentenced to six weeks in a convent for torturing a servant to death. Serfs were forbidden to appeal to the monarch for redress against a cruel noble. This had always been a somewhat theoretical right, but its loss meant, for instance, that the peasant had no legal way to object if his master chose to extend his *Barschina* (unpaid work). Catherine gave hundreds of thousands of serfs away as gifts to her lovers and successful generals. It was a cheap way to reward loyal service.

However, Catherine did make it legal for nobles to free their own serfs. She also introduced some minor improvements in conditions for Crown serfs, by setting up a number of schools for serf children, for instance. There is also some evidence that she considered issuing a Charter of the Peasants to go alongside her Charter of the Nobility and Charter of the Towns, setting down and defining the peasants' legal rights. But the few reforms she did make, although much praised by her Western European admirers and a few uncritical modern historians, were actually trivial. The Charter, if it ever existed, was never issued. In practice the serfs' condition worsened under Catherine, a sovereign who was theoretically in favour of helping them. Why did she not do more?

* The Pugachev Revolt of 1774–5 is usually given as the reason why Catherine turned her back on measures to improve the lot of the serfs. This revolt, led by an ex-soldier, Emilian Pugachev, was a mixture of serf rebellion and the last fight for freedom by the Cossacks, threatened by incorporation into Russia. Pugachev claimed to be Peter III, miraculously escaped from his evil 'wife'. Peasants could obey his invitation to rise up and kill their masters confident that a decree from their 'Tsar' made it all legal. The rising probably never had any chance of overthrowing Catherine as the vast majority of the rebels only wished to take over their land and had no intention of leaving their homes for a march on Moscow. As a result, although hundreds of thousands of peasants took part in the rebellion at one time or another, Pugachev never had enough men for his army. Yet the revolt was the most serious attempt to overthrow the system of government in over 100 years and was marked by great savagery on the part of the rebels. Nobles and officials were murdered, and several towns were captured. The first armies sent against Pugachev were defeated, and – perhaps most sinister of all – some of the troops, themselves conscripted peasants, changed sides and joined the rebels. All this was enough to frighten the nobles. The revolt was finally crushed and Pugachev was brought to Moscow in an iron cage. Today Soviet historians regard him as a hero and Intourist guides proudly show the square in Moscow where he was hanged. About 20 000 peasants had been killed in the battles before the nobles returned, and a futher unknown number were then butchered in revenge for the 2700 nobles, priests and government officials who had lost their lives during the revolt.

The Pugachev Revolt was the most serious attempt to overthrow the

Russian monarchy in the eighteenth century. It has been misunderstood by some historians who credit Pugachev with a far more modern, political motive for his revolt than he actually had. He was fighting to bring back a Russia which had passed, a Russia where the traditional religious customs would be restored, where foreigners would be expelled, where men would wear beards (as had been the custom before Peter the Great had started introducing his western reforms), and where the Cossacks would resume their old way of life. It was a reactionary rather than a revolutionary movement.

Its effects were certainly significant, however lightly Catherine might dismiss 'Monsieur Pugachev' in her letters to Voltaire. The revolt undobtedly increased social division and made both Catherine and the nobles aware of their dependence on each other. However, it was not the Pugachev Revolt which led Catherine to abandon her dreams of reducing serfdom. She had been extending serfdom since she came to power; the laws allowing nobles to punish serfs and banning serf appeals had been passed in 1765 and 1767. She continued this policy after Pugachev, concluding with the Charter of the Nobility. At the end of her reign there were nearly one million more serfs than there had been at the beginning. Catherine was well aware that she relied on the nobles to assist her in running the country; that abolishing or even reducing serfdom would entail enormous social upheaval and violent protests from the nobles; and that she lacked the administrative machinery and armed forces to enforce such a reform against their wishes. When Diderot grumbled that she should be doing more for the peasants, Catherine answered in a famous letter that shows how much her early idealism had become tempered by the realities of power:

1 You only work on paper, which endures all things, but I work on the human skin, which is irritable and ticklish.

Catherine's failure to help the peasants has been seen by sympathetic historians as the triumph of realism over naive theory. Her early optimism and high hopes for reform, as indicated by the *Nakaz* and the Free Economic Society, gradually gave way to the harsh realities of life in Russia. Even the most despotic of enlightened despots relied on the support of the nobles, and the experience of Joseph II was an object lesson to those who felt they could override the objections of nobles to reform. An alternative explanation is that her minor reforms and pious letters were all part of a clever scheme to persuade the *philosophes* that she cared about the peasants, whilst really she was far more interested in staying in power – and enjoying that power – than in any significant reforms. The fact that the conditions of the serfs worsened from the moment she became Tsarina makes this interpretation of her actions seem more likely.

However, both arguments make the mistake of assuming that

Catherine had the power to help the peasants if she wanted to. In practice, it is doubtful whether she ever had enough authority to impose reforms against the opposition of the nobles. She was well aware that politics is the art of the possible, and that in the eighteenth century the Russian nobles were not prepared to give up serfdom, a system which seemed so advantageous to them. It would not be until the nineteenth century, under the shock of military defeat, that a Russian Tsar would finally be able to abolish serfdom.

4 The Nobles

In contrast to the peasants, the status and privileges of the nobles improved considerably during Catherine's reign. However, the extent to which their *power* increased is open to question. There had been indications that nobles were gaining power at the expense of the Tsars since the death of Peter the Great. Their involvement in the various *coups* and their ability to persuade Anna and Peter III first to reduce and then to end state service were evidence of their greater assertiveness. In many ways Catherine seemed to continue this trend. A series of concessions to the nobles, including increasing their power to exploit the serfs in any way they chose, culminated in the Charter of the Nobility of 1785.

The Charter brought together existing laws and added some rights which were already custom but not yet law, as well as some new privileges. The result was a document which defined for the first time the rights and privileges of the nobles.

1.   The noble calling is the result of the qualities and virtues of men who held high office in the past, and distinguished themselves by their merits, by which they won for their descendants the noble appellation.
2.   It is not only useful for the empire but also just to preserve and establish the estate of nobility.
3.   The nobleman transmits his noble status to his wife and to his children.
8.   Without judicial proceedings no well-born person may lose noble status, his life or property.
12.   The well-born person may only be judged by his peers.
15.   Corporal punishment may not be inflicted on any well-born person.
17.   We guarantee independence and freedom to the Russian nobility for all time.
26–34.   Well-born persons are confirmed in their right to purchase villages, to sell what has been harvested in the villages, to possess, build and buy houses in the cities, to possess not only the surface of the lands belonging to them, but also whatever

minerals or plants may be present beneath the soil or water, and likewise all metals extracted from them, and in the right to possess forests and in the free use of these forests. They are permitted to have manufactories and industrial works, to sell products overseas and to export them.

35. In the villages, the house of the lord shall be exempt from military quartering.

36. The well-born person is freed from personal taxes.

In addition, nobles were exempted from certain punishments (but could be executed or deprived of their status for serious crimes) and could not have their property confiscated. Nobles could have their own assembly in each *guberniya* (province), could stand for election for various posts in the province, and could make their views known to the governor (appointed by Catherine) or to the Empress herself. Finally, each Provincial Assembly chose a leader, the Marshal, who was responsible for drawing up and keeping up to date the register of nobles. Strict rules were laid down governing who could claim noble status.

* The Charter is clearly an important document, but there is some disagreement as to where its importance lies. It could be seen as a major victory for the nobles, as the culmination of 60 years of steady improvement in their status, wealth and power. It could be argued that they now had a protected, exclusive role in society and controlled local affairs through their assemblies. Amongst the new privileges were those relating to exclusive control over minerals and those protecting their legal rights and property. Even decisions about who could call himself a noble were now completely in their hands.

Catherine would not have seen it that way. To her the Charter meant that there was now a firm legal basis for the social structure in Russia, instead of the archaic social system of Peter the Great. For a ruler intent on giving Russia an enlightened and rational system of government, this was a necessity. The new privileges and concessions were minor ones. The Charter did not, in itself, increase noble power over serfs. Instead it confirmed the existing relationship between noble and serf. Very little in the Charter was in fact new. It confirmed rights first issued in 1762 or which were already common practice. Even the noble assemblies were not new. They had existed since 1775, although their powers had not been properly defined at that stage. Most importantly, however, Catherine would argue that she had not given away any significant power, since it was still the governor, appointed by her, who made all noteworthy decisions at a local level. Treasure sums up her achievement: 'skillfully Catherine presented them with the semblance of government . . . she preserved the real power of those she chose, the Governors'.

Catherine was pleased with the Charter. The threat of a noble *coup* had been reduced. The nobles had been given what they wanted – privilege and status – whilst she had ensured that no power of any significance had fallen into their hands. The nobles worked now as willing junior partners to the government, rather than the unwilling servants of Peter I. She ended up identifying herself mainly with her nobles. 'I am' she admitted cheerfully 'an aristocrat by profession'. Whether the peasants would have been so pleased with her achievements is, of course, another matter.

5 Economic Policy

Catherine had clear ideas about economics but, characteristically, was prepared to use different economic theories as they suited her best. She aimed to promote the economic development of Russia, and was particularly interested in measures that could increase the country's population and supply of materials needed for war.

In general she favoured the development of free trade. Early in her reign she confirmed Peter III's decrees abolishing monopolies and reducing import and export duties. In the *Nakaz* Catherine pointed to England as a good example of the benefits of free trade. Both in 1767 and, more extensively in 1782, she altered customs duties in favour of free trade. By the end of her reign all exports and many imports were duty-free, and even the duty on luxury imports had been cut from 200 to 20 per cent.

These actions, along with a steady development in industry, the signing of several bilateral trade agreements with other European states, and the opening up of ports such as Odessa following the wars with Turkey, led to a growth in trade from 21 million roubles a year in 1762 to 96 million roubles a year at her death. However, despite some successful attempts to develop a Russian merchant fleet, much of this trade was still carried in foreign ships. Some attempt to solve the perennial problem of communications was made by the building of a small number of new roads and canals, but this problem remained a major obstacle to Russian economic development.

In common with several other rulers, Catherine encouraged skilled immigrants with promises of free land and tax exemptions for up to 30 years. Significant numbers of Germans accepted the offer and settled in the Volga region, where they were to form a close-knit and successful community until Stalin wiped them out in the 1940s.

If Catherine's attempts to encourage trade and immigration were generally successful, she fared less well in her financial policies and in her attempts to develop industry and technology. At first Catherine's finances appeared healthy. There was an attempt to lighten the burden on peasants by reducing the Salt Tax whilst increasing the liquor duties, which hit the rich more. However, Catherine's wars and court expenditure meant that by 1794 Russia was facing a financial crisis.

Catherine rejected the option of placing direct taxes on the nobles. Instead she increased the poll tax (the main tax paid by the peasants), as well as a range of indirect taxes. Madariaga defends her actions on the grounds that as a *percentage of their income*, peasants were paying no more in poll tax in 1795 than they were in 1762. It is also true that, compared to other states such as Prussia and France, only a relatively small percentage of expenditure – less than 30 per cent – went to the armed forces, whilst a high proportion went on local administration and services. This defence of Catherine can be taken too far; taxes went up in the 1790s because of a series of aggressive wars, and because Catherine spent a significant amount – some 12 per cent of her expenditure – on her court and her favourites. This was a proportion that not even the notoriously extravagant Louis XV of France ever spent on Versailles and his mistresses.

Despite such initiatives as the foundation of a Mining Academy, little was done to develop new methods for Russian industry. The reluctance of factory owners to adopt new technology is typified by the failure of the inventor Pulzanov to find buyers for his steam engine, whilst at the same time a similar machine, invented separately by James Watt in England, was making both its inventor and the country richer. With a reliance on the cheap but inefficient labour of industrial serfs, there could be no industrial revolution in Russia. Despite some growth in factories and in urban population, Russian industry was falling further behind that of Western Europe, rather than catching up. Similarly, Catherine's attempts to foster greater freedom for town councils by the proclamation of a Charter of Towns (1785) at the same time as her Charter of the Nobility, failed, since the new Town Councils had no income and were dependent on the co-operation of the Governor.

Catherine bequeathed to her successors a healthy trade balance, but also serious financial problems and an inefficient and declining industry. She had probably achieved as much as she could, given the restrictions that serfdom and Russian geography placed on her, but her relative failure in the economic sphere merely underlines the extent to which the continued existence of serfdom was holding Russia back.

6 Religion

Enlightened Despots were expected to practise religious toleration. This was one area in which Catherine had no difficulty in satisfying the wishes of the *philosophes*. She had been brought up as a Lutheran, but had changed easily enough to the Orthodox Church in order to please the Russian people. It would seem that she had no strong religious feelings herself and was prepared to joke about religion in letters to her cynical friends, but was always careful to show herself to be outwardly pious for the people. It was a small price to pay for their attention.

It would therefore not be difficult for her to support religious toleration and a reduction in the power of the state church. In any event, this policy was nothing new in Russia. Peter I had granted toleration to Protestants and Catholics in order to encourage western Europeans to come to Russia, so there was no surprise when this policy was continued. What was new was the toleration Catherine granted to Muslims and the rather grudging concessions to the Jews. These included giving them equal rights (in theory) in towns to stand for municipal office. She also granted toleration to the Old Believers, the branch of the Eastern Orthodox Church that had broken away from the mainstream church in the seventeenth century and which still had large numbers of followers amongst the peasantry.

Catherine had various motives for extending toleration. Her own enlightened ideas were important, but it was also expedient for the development of Russia. It was already a long established custom, both to practise religious toleration and to assert state control over the various churches. Article 494 in the *Nakaz* advocated religious toleration, not for 'enlightened' reasons, but to prevent public disorder in a multi-cultural empire. Whatever Catherine's motives, the result was that by the end of her reign Russia was one of the few countries in Europe where there was no religious persecution at all.

An action that came as a surprise to many was the confirmation of Peter III's seizure of Church lands. This was one of the reasons Peter had lost his throne in 1762. Yet only two years later Catherine was able to confirm the decree, although at the time of Peter's decree she had indicated her opposition to it. Probably she had always appreciated the benefits that would result from a seizure of Church lands, but in 1762 it had been expedient to oppose it. The decree in 1764 greatly weakened the power of the Church. Possibly Catherine did this partly for 'enlightened' reasons, but at the same time she enriched herself with nearly one million serfs (many later given away to her favourites) and money. The Bishop of Rostov protested at the action and was gaoled for life. Other Church leaders did not protest. Catherine gave the Church money instead, but this could not disguise the fact that priests were now little more than salaried servants of the state. The fact that the Church's power had been so seriously weakened 60 years before by Peter I helps to explain its inability to resist Catherine's take-over of its lands.

Writers such as Voltaire judged Catherine's religious policy a success. Enlightened ideas, a lack of personal religious commitment by Catherine and practical politics had all combined to make Russia a country of genuine religious toleration.

7 Education

Catherine's interest in education seems to have come in two phases – in the 1760s and the 1780s. There can be no doubt that she had a real interest in the subject, but her achievements were very limited.

In 1763 she founded Russia's first medical college, and set a brave example by allowing herself to be innoculated against smallpox. She revived the Academy of Science, started a parallel Academy of Fine Arts, and reformed the Military Academy. These gave some indication of her interest, but were of symbolic rather than practical importance for Russian education since they were only attended by small numbers of students. In 1764 she founded Russia's first girls' school, the Smolny Institute, in fine buildings on the outskirts of St. Petersburg. This exclusive institution for noble girls (with a few middle class girls who had different uniforms) gave them a strictly regimented but up-to-date education. Catherine, who had the benefit of a formal education herself in Germany, had a natural interest in girls' education.

It is easy to be dismissive about the effects of these measures, which did nothing for the education of most Russians. However, Catherine was also interested in state schools for all. This concept was included as an ideal in the *Nakaz*, and an Education Commission was set to work to suggest the best method to introduce a state education system into Russia. Taking advice from Austria, which had the most extensive state education system at that time, Catherine established Russia's first teacher training college in 1783. This was followed by a decree in 1786 establishing a system of free state education. Schools were co-educational – a most unusual feature at this time – but were not available to the children of serfs. It was not compulsory to send children to school and many nobles preferred not to have their children mix with those from lower classes, paying instead for private education. A detailed and modern curriculum was laid down. Catherine's decree also abolished corporal punishment, making Russia the first country to try to manage without canings (although there is evidence that most teachers ignored this part of the decree). To encourage people to become teachers, it was made possible for them to achieve noble status after 22 years of good service. They were expected to be 'Christian, honourable, loving, bold, patient, hard-working and unprejudiced'. On the other hand they could be dismissed for drunkenness – a widespread problem among Russian teachers at this time.

The results were disappointing. With just two per cent of government expenditure allocated to education, only some 300 schools were built by 1796. All of these were in towns and catered exclusively for the middle classes. A few peasants had the opportunity to send their children to schools run by their masters, but the vast majority of serf children had no formal education at all. In theory, thanks to a decree from Catherine, a serf could become a member of the Academy of Science, but in practice none could hope to achieve this.

Catherine herself rejected the idea of extending schools to the villages. One reason may have been the vast extra expense this would have involved, along with the shortage of trained teachers. However, this was probably not her main objection to educating the serfs. She was also opposed to such schools on principle, and towards the end of her reign confided that she did not agree with educating serfs.

1 The *canille* [rabble] must not be educated to the point where they know as much as you or I, and refuse to obey us.

Her early idealism, shown in her advocating schools for all in the *Nakaz*, was replaced over the years by greater realism and closer identification with the wishes of the nobles.

Despite their limited scope, Catherine's reforms were still well ahead of those in many other countries. When she died only Austria had a more extensive state school system than Russia. England was still 70 years away from its first state school. Given the immense problems involved in establishing a state education system, she had actually done rather more than most of the Enlightened Despots.

8 Government

Amongst Catherine's reforms were the changes she made in government. The idea of reforming Peter I's cumbersome system of provinces was not new. A Commission working for the Empress Elizabeth had recommended major changes in the 1750s. The delegates to the *Zemstvo* had made many complaints about the inefficiency and corruption of the existing system of local government. However, Catherine did not act until the Pugachev Revolt revealed the fragility of the system.

Many of Pugachev's early successes were due to the collapse of local administration. The ending of the revolt was quickly followed by a decree of 1775 which established 50 *gubernii* (provinces), each of approximately 800 000 inhabitants, to be controlled by a governor appointed by an answerable to the Empress. Each province was sub-divided into *uezdy* (districts). The *gubernii* and *uezdy* were far more manageable in size than Peter's huge provinces, and for the first time Russia was given an effective form of local government which was to last until 1917 – the longest lasting of Catherine's reforms. At the same time provision was made for the governor to be assisted by a board of local government, civil servants and a system of courts. Each province also had an elected noble assembly to give guidance to the governor, although its exact powers were not defined until the Charter of the Nobility eleven years later.

The governor had extensive responsibilities, including maintaining law and order, tax collection, control of the army, education, health and transport. There was a considerable expansion in the number of people employed in local government, from 13 000 before the reform to 27 000 in 1796, while the cost of local administration rose from 1.7 million roubles a year in 1774 to nearly 11 million in 1796. These statistics indicate the high priority Catherine gave to local administration. Russia now enjoyed a system of local government which was probably as efficient as those in western Europe. The fact that there were no major serf revolts after 1775, despite the steadily worsening position of the peasants, is evidence of the new system's success.

However, the success was not complete. Catherine never overcame the problem of the lack of honest, trained civil servants. Examples of corruption continued, although on a much smaller scale, as they have ever since in Russia. Yet Catherine had achieved a reasonably effective system of local government and at the same time made it much harder for people to rebel against the monarchy. In theory at least, the increasing work of local government in building hospitals and roads improved the lives of ordinary Russians. The average peasant might feel these reforms were a mixed blessing, since it was the same efficient government that maintained law and order, conscripted the peasants for the army and took much of their income in taxes. But whatever grumbles the peasants might have, there is no doubt that Catherine's system of local government was an improvement on Peter the Great's chaos.

9 The Last Years

Any discussion of Catherine's achievements must also include consideration of the reversals that occurred in her later years. During the last five years of her life she became increasingly reactionary. A number of explanations have been offered for this: that she was ageing; that she had fallen under the spell of the last of her more than 20 lovers – the young, ruthless and unpleasant Plato Zubov who strongly opposed enlightened ideas; that her years of power had corrupted her; that she who had once been the outsider with bright ideas had now become more aristocratic than the aristocrats; and that she had been frightened by the French Revolution, whose outbreak in 1789 horrified her. The impact of the French Revolution was perhaps the most important of these since of all the European rulers, she had the most recent experience of a popular uprising and was well aware that the danger of revolt remained. All the rulers of the *ancien régime* feared that the Revolution might spread its doctrines throughout Europe. Catherine took the lead in denouncing the Revolution and with it anything or anyone who seemed to be on France's side or who supported the ideas issuing from Paris.

Catherine, who in earlier years had encouraged young nobles to go abroad to receive the most liberal education from universities in Germany, France and Britain, now tried to cut Russia off from all contact with France. All Russian students were recalled, French people in Russia were expelled unless they swore an oath condemning the Revolution, and press censorship was introduced. In these ways

'Europe watches whilst Catherine II conquers'

Catherine hoped to insulate the Russian people from any awareness that in France the ordinary people had overthrown their king and were taking away the land from the nobles. Her own *Nakaz*, which in earlier years had been ordered to be read aloud every year to officials in local government and which had been on sale in bookshops, was now withdrawn.

No doubt most nobles were as shocked as Catherine by the Revolution. However, a few had taken seriously the enlightened theories which were taught at European universities. One of these, Alexander Radishchev, published a book with the harmless title *A Journey from St Petersburg to Moscow* in 1790. It included a bitter attack on the evils of serfdom, called on the government to abolish the institution, and in a famous prophecy warned that if serfdom was not quickly abolished there would be bloody revolution in Russia.

1 Do you not know what destruction threatens us, and in what peril
   we stand? A stream that is barred in its course becomes more
   powerful in proportion to the opposition it meets. Once it bursts
   the dam, nothing can stem the flood. Such are our brothers, who
5 we keep in chains. They are waiting for a favourable time and

place. The alarm bells ring. The destructive forces break loose
with terrifying speed. Round about us we see sword and poison.
Death and fiery desolation will be the result of our harshness and
inhumanity. The more stubborn we are in loosening the fetters,
10 the more violent will be their revenge. Recall how deception
roused the slaves to destroy their masters. They hastened to
follow a crude pretender. They killed their masters. They sought
more the joy of revenge than the benefit of broken shackles. This
is what awaits us, what we must expect.

These were ideas Catherine herself had claimed to support in the 1760s.
Now she was horrified by the book and declared that it was 'worse than
Pugachev'. It is a measure of her fear that she should consider a book
which would only be read by a few thousand educated people a greater
threat to her than the Pugachev Revolt. Radishchev was arrested and
sentenced to death, a sentence which Catherine graciously reduced to
ten years in Siberia.

In 1792 a better known writer, Novikov, was sentenced to 15 years
imprisonment. Novikov was a supporter of Freemasonry, a movement
Catherine suspected of having links with the Revolution. He was also
accused of maintaining secret links with Catherine's son Paul, who was
known to oppose aspects of his mother's rule. Once upon a time
Catherine had herself contributed to Novikov's satirical magazine, but
that did not save him now. These two punishments show Catherine at
her worst; intolerant and ruthless towards those who dared to criticise
her or the system over which she presided.

 * When comparing Catherine's achievements with the fine phrases of
the *Nakaz*, it is easy to paint her as a hypocrite who wrote fine words to
win praise from sycophatic western *philosophes* while actually running
Russia as an old-fashioned despot. Nor does she come out well when
one looks at the none too modest epitaph that she proposed for herself
some time before she died:

1 Here lies Catherine II, born at Stettin in 1729. She went to Russia
  in 1744 to marry Peter III. At the age of fourteen she made the
  triple resolution to please her husband, Elizabeth and the nation.
  She neglected nothing in trying to achieve this. Eighteen years of
5 solitude gave her the opportunity to read many books. She
  desired nothing but the best for her country and tried to give her
  subjects happiness, liberty and wealth. She forgave easily and
  hated no one. Tolerant, undemanding and gay, she had a
  republican spirit and a kind heart. She had good friends.

It is not difficult to point to many parts both of this document and the
Nakaz where Catherine lamentably failed to achieve the high ideals
which she had set out for herself. There is no doubt that she enjoyed the

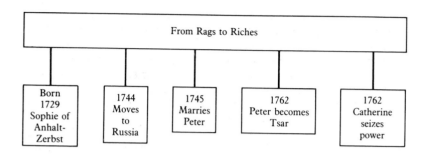

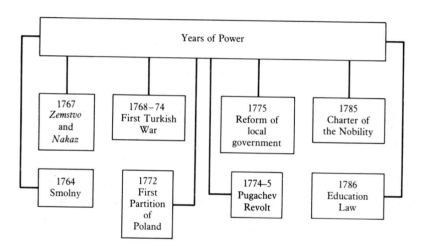

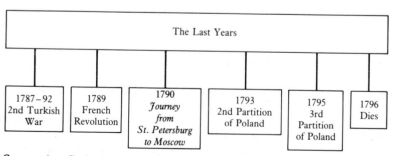

Summary – Catherine the Great

adulation of the *philosophes* and encouraged them to portray Russia, quite misleadingly, as a country run purely on enlightened lines. It is also true that as she grew older she increasingly distanced herself from her own earlier enlightened ideas. Nevertheless, one should not underestimate her real achievements which turned Russia from the arbitrary semi-military state of Peter the Great to a country with a proper legal and administrative framework. Catherine was the first ruler in Russia for a long time to have a vision of a more efficiently-run country and to be willing to try new methods. She did start down the road of 'consultation', although it was an experiment she never repeated. She enjoyed intellectual debate and corresponded with famous writers, not just so that they should glorify her name in Europe, but also for the stimulation of sharing ideas with other intellectuals. She gave the élite cultural freedom, at least until 1789. She reduced the role of the army in Russian society – under Peter I it had dominated all aspects of Russian government – and only a lack of trained honest civil servants prevented her from achieving a total overhaul of local administration.

Her failure to do anything worthwhile to help the peasants and her attempts to turn the clock back after 1789 are the most serious criticisms of Catherine as a reformer. The interpretation that she genuinely wanted to help the peasants but was prevented from doing so by the power of the nobles is probably invalid. It was during her early years as ruler than she put forward her most radical suggestions for reform in the *Nakaz*, but it was at this time that she was most vulnerable to being overthrown. In her later years, when her position was safe, she made no attempt to help the serfs. It seems more likely that her increasing awareness of just how difficult it would be to abolish serfdom in general, and the Pugachev Revolt in particular, convinced her that the time was not yet right.

Catherine's achievement is best seen when contrasting her reign with those of her predecessors and her successors. Madariaga sums up her achievement this way: 'It was a time when despotism was turned into monarchy, when men obeyed through honour, not fear'.

Making notes on 'Catherine the Great'

Again in this chapter you should be less concerned with simply describing what Catherine did than in deciding (i) to what extent her policies were influenced by the Enlightenment. You will need to be able to identify (ii) those factors which put her in a weaker position than some other monarchs to introduce reforms. At the end you should feel confident about answering the question, (iii) 'Was she a genuine reformer who was unable to achieve more because of reistance from the nobles, or a hypocrite who never intended any reforms anyway – or is there an alternative explanation between these two extremes?'

The following headings may help with your notes:

1.   Coming to Power (This section is background and only needs very brief notes)
1.1. The Legacy of Peter the Great
1.2. How Catherine came to power
1.3. Russia in 1762
2.   *Zemstvo* and *Nakaz*
2.1. Motives for summoning the *Zemstvo*
2.2. Composition and purpose of the *Zemstvo*
2.3. Purpose of the *Nakaz*
2.4. Reception of the *Nakaz*
2.5. Content and interpretations of the *Nakaz*
2.6. Assessment of Catherine and the *Zemstvo*

(In sections 3–8 below concentrate on Catherine's aims and achievements, and avoid merely listing the different 'things that she did'.)

3.   Serfdom
3.1. The Pugachev Revolt
4.   The Nobles
4.1. Significance of The Charter of the Nobility
5.   Economic Policy
6.   Religion
7.   Education
8.   Government
9.   The Last Years
9.1. The impact of the French Revolution on Catherine
9.2. Assessment

Answering essay questions on 'Catherine the Great'

Catherine II is a popular topic among examiners. Sometimes you will be asked to compare her achievements with those of another enlightened despot: such questions will be discussed on page 159. For the moment we will concentrate on questions that are solely about Catherine. These often start with a quotation which you are expected to discuss. Quotations, particularly long ones, may appear formidable at first. Look at the following examples:

1.   ' "Reality weighed more heavily with her than ideas." Comment on this view of Catherine the Great.'

2. 'Consider the view that the policies of Catherine the Great served the interests of the nobles rather than those of the crown.'
3. '"Catherine II – misnamed the Great," Discuss.'
4. '"For an obscure German princess to make herself Empress of Russia was no mean achievement, but for Catherine II to remain Empress for more than 30 years and to die a natural death was probably a greater one." Discuss.'
5. '"The limitations of her power and freedom of action allowed her little scope to exercise her genuinely enlightened views." Discuss this view of Catherine II's domestic policies.'
6. '"Russia's debt to her was immense, and all the more remarkable because she was not Russian." To what extent and for what reasons was Russia indebted to Catherine II?'

'Challenging statement' questions, although often unpopular with candidates, actually help the student by offering guidance on what aspects of Catherine's reign are to be covered, and by offering one possible interpretation to discuss. The first task, therefore, is to identify the aspects of Catherine's reign in which the examiner is interested. Question 2, for instance, is clearly concerned with the *effects* of Catherine's policies. Make a list of the aspects of her reign which are being asked about in the other five questions.

When the examiner offers his own interpretation, as in 'challenging statement' questions, some candidates make the mistake of thinking that they are expected to agree with this viewpoint, and only present evidence that supports it. Actually, the examiner will be hoping for a more balanced approach, with arguments both for and against the particular line, and some judgement at the end.

You have a three-stage process to undertake when you tackle a 'challenging statement' question:

a) Identify the aspect(s) of the topic being asked about
b) Identify the point of view being put forward by the examiner
c) Identify what other arguments or aspects you will need to include in order to answer the question.

It would now be worth your while to devise essay plans using this three-stage approach with some of the other questions listed above.

Source-based questions on 'Catherine the Great'

1 Catherine and her reputation
Read the extracts from the two letters from Voltaire to Catherine on page 65 and study the cartoon of Catherine on page 80. Answer the following questions:

a)   What is meant by 'freedom of conscience' (page 65 line 6)?
                                                          (2 marks)
b)   What do the letters tell us about (i) Voltaire's character, and
     (ii) Voltaire's aims?   (4 marks)
c)   What do the letters tell us about (i) Catherine's character, and (ii)
     Catherine's aims?   (4 marks)
d)   Explain the ways in which the cartoon's image of Catherine is at
     variance with that put forward by Voltaire.   (4 marks)
e)   For what reasons and with what success did Catherine attempt to
     gain the support of people like Voltaire?   (6 marks)

2 The Nakaz and the Charter of the Nobility

Read the extracts from the *Nakaz* on pages 65–6 and the extract
from the Charter of the Nobility on pages 72–3. You will also need to
refer back to the Beccaria extract on page 22. Answer the following
questions:

a)   Explain what is meant by 'Russia is a European State' (page 65
     Article 6), 'The Commission (page 66 Article 522) and 'Military
     Quartering' (page 75 Article 35).   (6 marks)
b)   What evidence is there that parts of the *Nakaz* derive directly
     from Beccaria's book? Support your answer with
     quotations.   (4 marks)
c)   In what ways do the articles of the Charter contradict those in the
     Nakaz? Support your answer with quotations.   (4 marks)
d)   Which of the two documents was the more significant for Russia?
     Explain your answer.   (6 marks)

3 Assessing Catherine II's achievements

Read the extract from *Journey From St Petersburg to Moscow* on pages
80–1 and Catherine's epitaph on page 81. Answer the following
questions:

a)   Explain what is meant by 'our brothers' (page 80 line 4), 'a crude
     pretender' (page 81 line 12), and 'eighteen years of solitude'
     (page 81 line 4).   (6 marks)
b)   What does Catherine's epitaph tell us about her character and
     achievements?   (4 marks)
c)   How and why does Radishchev's assessment of Catherine's
     achievements disagree with those of Catherine herself? (4 marks)
d)   Of what value are these two sources to a historian studying the
     reign of Catherine II?   (6 marks)

CHAPTER 5

Joseph II

1 Early Life

When Empress Maria Theresa of Austria gave birth to her longed-for son and heir in March 1741, naming him Joseph in honour of one of the saints she revered most, couriers were sent to inform the courts of Europe as was normal. Within a few weeks, however, far more dramatic news was coming out of Austria. The Prussians, to general surprise, had won the Battle of Mollwitz, ensuring that they would keep the province of Silesia. At the age of three months, baby Joseph was presented to the Hungarian Diet as Maria Theresa made an impassioned plea to the nobles to support her with money and men against Frederick of Prussia. Already as a baby Joseph was involved in the two problems that would dominate his life: the aggression of Frederick II and the Austrian monarchy's reliance on powerful nobles and assemblies. Joseph was to spend his reign (1780–90) trying to combat both of these threats to the power and integrity of the Austrian monarchy.

It was a struggle he was to lose. In the process he become one of the most controversial monarchs in Austrian history. At the end of his reign Joseph believed that he had been a total failure, and many historians have agreed with this gloomy judgment. It is the reasons for Joseph's failure which have aroused the most discussion. Was it his enlightened aims which led to his failure, or was it the methods he employed to try to achieve his aims? If the former, does this prove that Enlightened Despotism was unworkable in a state like Austria? If the latter, to what extent were his faulty methods the results of defects in his own character, and to what extent were they caused by the inheritance left by Maria Theresa?

Maria Theresa's reign (1740–80) was dominated by the threat of war with Prussia and the problems of running her large and complex empire. She managed to combine this with looking after her large family – she had sixteen children in all, and most survived to adulthood. Unusually for the time, she spent some time each day with her children and carefully supervised their education. In Joseph's case this was particularly important, since he was heir to the throne and she was determined that he should be properly trained for his responsibilities.

* Yet despite her care, and the unusual instructions to the tutors to ensure that the lessons were enjoyable, Joseph disliked his schooling and was constantly being criticised by his teachers for being idle. He took little interest in most subjects, enjoying only mathematics and foreign languages. He showed an aversion to the subjects which were a major part of the education of princes in the eighteenth century. He disliked dancing, music, art and literature, and was particularly opposed to hunting which, he claimed, 'serves as an excuse to neglect serious occupations'.

It was not long before he was reading the works of the *philosophes*, although his mother disapproved of these authors. He appears to have absorbed many of the enlightened theories that were fashionable at the time. He knew the works of Voltaire and was impressed by the *Encyclopédie* and the Physiocrats. Perhaps the writer who most influenced him was Martini, the Professor of Law at Vienna University. Martini, who also influenced Joseph's brother Leopold, stressed the supremacy of Natural Law over Church Law. Joseph liked what he read, but he was careful to distance himself from the famous French writers. Monarchs such as Frederick II and Catherine II might go out of their way to be seen with, or to have regular correspondence with writers such as Voltaire and Diderot, but Joseph never tried to cultivate a personal relationship with them. During his early years there was a good reason for this: his mother forbade him. Maria Theresa was strongly opposed to the Enlightenment and refused to have the works of Voltaire or the other *philosophes* published in Austria. She summed up her attitude with the words 'I do not permit the introduction into this country of such horrible books, which serve neither science, pleasure nor religion'. Against such strongly held views, Joseph dared not argue as long as his mother lived.

Joseph made no personal contact with any of the writers, even after the death of his mother in 1780. His reluctance to meet them reflects his preference for talking to people who were intellectually his inferior. He was never interested in turning his court into a forum for intelligent discussion as Frederick and Catherine had done. Nor was he interested in using the *philosophes* for propaganda purposes.

Contemporaries held varying opinions about how much of the Enlightenment Joseph had absorbed. Catherine II was very impressed with him when they met for the first time in 1780, writing that he had 'the best informed mind I have ever met'. This would seem to be high praise from one of the most intelligent and sophisticated rulers in Europe, but since she was at the time interested in making an alliance with Austria, the flattery was probably as insincere as that which she exchanged with Voltaire. Frederick II, who met Joseph in 1769, was not impressed, describing him as lacking in patience and as having received only a superficial education. He also commented that Joseph had no real ideas of his own, and this seems justified. Joseph absorbed and used many of the ideas of the *philosophes*, but, unlike Frederick and Catherine, never wrote any books himself.

He gave some encouragement to the development of drama by establishing a German theatre, but in other respects showed no interest in supporting the arts. He had a certain aptitude for music, but treated

Austria's greatest composer, Mozart, shabbily. If one of the criteria for the successful Enlightened Despot was to be seen to patronise the arts and sciences, then Joseph clearly did not fit. His narrow range of interests, caring neither for the royal male's traditional pursuits of hunting and women, nor for the more recent fashion of patronising the arts, marks him out as one of the most isolated and lonely of eighteenth-century monarchs.

* There was one interest which Joseph took up at an early age and

Joseph II as a young man

which he enjoyed throughout his reign – travel. He was, in fact, the first Austrian ruler to visit all the provinces of his far-flung empire, and he also travelled extensively abroad. Everywhere he went he travelled incognito, staying in hotels and mixing with ordinary people. His informal approach to his subjects, his willingness to discuss their problems with them on equal terms, and his amusement if his real identity was discovered, is one of his most attractive features. Some other Enlightened Despots shared his dislike for the pomp and ceremonies of royal rituals, but none were as free and open in their dealings with their subjects. Joseph loved meeting ordinary people and talking to them. As a result of these talks he was far better informed, and was far more sympathetic towards, the ordinary people of his empire than other monarchs who professed great concern for their subjects' welfare.

Travel also enabled him to judge his fellow monarchs at first hand. Between 1769 and 1780 he made three foreign journeys, meeting Frederick II in 1769, Louis XVI of France in 1777 and Catherine II in 1780. The first two journeys achieved little of practical value. His visit to Russia in 1780 was the only one with political significance, for there is no doubt that this meeting helped pave the way for the break-up of the alliance between Russia and Prussia and its replacement by one between Russia and Austria. At the time Joseph felt he had achieved a diplomatic *coup* by isolating Frederick and gaining a powerful ally; events were to prove that Russia would be the only winner from the switch of alliances.

* The relationship between Joseph and his mother had not been an easy one. While other Enlightened Despots had succeeded to their thrones when relatively young, Joseph had to wait 40 years to become Emperor. Maria Theresa, anxious to train her successor, had given Joseph some responsibilities but had ensured that he had little real power. As the years went by he found these restrictions increasingly irksome, and there were frequent disagreements between mother and son. Prince Kaunitz, Maria Theresa's Chief Minister and the architect of the Franco-Austrian alliance, found that he had to use all his diplomatic skills to prevent a total breach between the Empress and her heir. Yet at the same time Joseph was fond of his mother and seems to have been genuinely heart-broken when late in 1780 news came of her death.

Maria Theresa's reign, and Joseph's whole life, were dominated by Frederick the Great. In a bloodless campaign in 1740 Frederick conquered Silesia, and at the same time threatened Austria's position as a Great Power and as the dominant state in Germany. For the next 23 years Maris Theresa used both diplomacy and war to try to regain her lost province. None of this worked against the military genius of Frederick. By 1763 she was forced to admit defeat.

* In the process of organising her state for war against Prussia, Maria

Theresa had been obliged to modernise the system of government. The patchwork of separate states which made up the Habsburg Empire lost some of their independence, although Hungary and the Austrian Netherlands retained Diets with important powers. Some of the Provincial Estates lost their control over taxes. Instead of voting the government its taxes every year, they were voted once every ten years. In addition, a start was made on taxing the nobles and clergy. There was predictably strong opposition to these reforms, which in the end applied only in Austria and Bohemia. At the same time Austrian civil servants were extending their responsibilities in the provinces. At first they were only responsible for recruiting soldiers and collecting taxes. In time they were also placed in charge of road-building and education. In 1749 Maria Theresa established the *Directorium* to administer the combined provinces of Austria and Bohemia. For the first time these two provinces were now directly under the control of the Empress. It is typical of Maria Theresa's caution that she made no attempt to centralise the other provinces. Until 1780 much of the Habsburg Empire owed only nominal allegiance to Vienna. In particular, Hungary, which made up nearly half the Habsburg lands, was virtually self-governing and untouched by her reforms. Maria Theresa, facing the more urgent task of fighting off Prussia, left the reform of Hungary for later generations to tackle.

Reforms were made in the central government. A series of councils, such as the *Directorium* and the Chamber of Finance, worked under a new Council of State at which Maria Theresa met with her senior ministers.

A start was also made on reforming the curriculum at the universities, where the Jesuits had previously exercised control. Theology lost its dominant position, to be replaced by subjects which would be more useful for a career in the bureaucracy – Law, accounts, and politics. For the first time non-Catholics could go to university. Educational reforms also reached the ordinary people. The establishment of a Ministry of Education indicated the priority Maria Theresa attached to this field and the curriculum was broadened in state schools to include history, geography, mathematics and German, along with the traditional subjects of religious education and Latin.

   * There was nothing enlightened about Maria Theresa's reforms. They were designed to strengthen the state in the face of foreign aggression – not because she felt that a strong and caring state was itself a desirable end. Maria Theresa was an extremely cautious ruler who was reluctant to make changes except when absolutely necessary. In particular she was careful not to disturb the privileges and power of the nobles or the Church. She believed that change should come slowly and was realistic as to what could be attained during her lifetime. For these reasons her reforms, although limited, were largely successful.

Maria Theresa, far from having any sympathy with the Enlightenment, was openly hostile to it. As well as having the works of the *philosophes* banned, she showed herself to be a bigoted reactionary in religious affairs. She allowed the Roman Catholic Church to retain most of its wealth and power, and actively persecuted the Jews, declaring 'I know of no worse plague for the state than this race of deceivers'. Protestants were treated little better, and she announced that 'I shall not be led by any spirit of toleration'.

Her reluctance to antagonise the nobles led her to adopt a half-hearted and ineffective approach to the problem of serfdom. She was well aware of the difficulties confronted by her peasants and was advised by some of her ministers and her son to abolish serfdom entirely, if only for the economic advantages that a free peasantry would bring to Austria. The serfs working on crown lands were allowed to rent their own land, but Maria Theresa did little for those owned by nobles. What appeared to be an important law of 1770 allowing peasants to buy their own land from their masters was simply ignored by the nobles. Maria Theresa failed to tackle effectively the most important social and economic problem Austria faced.

When Maria Theresa died in 1780 her old adversary Frederick II commented that 'she was a credit to her sex'; this patronising remark was, in fact, high praise by Frederick's standards, and he added 'A new order of things begin', as he wondered how he would cope with her less predictable son. The unease about how Joseph would run his empire without the restraining hand of his mother was also shared by others. In his 40 years of apprenticeship as Emperor, Joseph had already showed signs of being a ruthless and single-minded person who would tolerate no opposition. Now at last he could put his ideas into practice.

2 Political Philosophy

Joseph's unusually long apprenticeship in politics was undoubtedly one of the reasons for his intolerance of opposition and his desire to see instant results from his reforms. For 15 long years, between 1765 and 1780, he was given impressive-sounding titles but little real power. He saw the best years of his life slip by whilst his mother failed to make what he considered to be long-overdue reforms. When at last Maria Theresa died in 1780, Joseph's grief at her death was mixed with relief that he could now exercise full power. However, he was suffering from bouts of ill-health himself and may have thought that his time was likely to be short. In just a few years he would have to make up for the decades wasted by his mother.

Joseph had a clear vision of the state he wished to create. There were three major influences on the development of his political philosophy. First, and arguably the most important, was the influence of Frederick the Great. Joseph was both fascinated and repelled by Frederick. On the one hand he was clearly Austria's most dangerous and skillful adversary, a ruler who continued to threaten Austria until his death in 1786. On the other hand Joseph admired him. Here was a king who, it appeared, had transformed weak and scattered lands into a strong, unitary state. He was a king who ruled for the benefit of his people and who strengthened his state through cynical diplomacy and war. Frederick was, in short, the ideal king, and one whose achievements Joseph wished to emulate. He saw himself as being in a similar position to the rulers of Prussia in trying to unify and centralise scattered lands. Much of Joseph's impatience can be explained by his perception of the time Austria had wasted whilst Prussia continued to build up her strength. By the time he reached supreme power in 1780, Prussia had been given some 70 years start. Joseph feared that unless Austria rapidly made up for this lost time, Prussia would eventually destroy the Austrian Empire. Unfortunately, in his haste to copy Prussia, Joseph underrated both the length of time Prussian rulers had taken to strengthen their state, and Frederick's care in maintaining a partnership with the nobles.

The second major factor influencing Joseph's political philosophy was the Enlightenment. Joseph believed in the idea of a social contract between ruler and people. Since all individuals and social groups were, by definition, selfish, only the monarch could do what was best for the nation as a whole. All power was granted to the King in the social contract, provided that he used it solely for the benefit of his people and the state. No individual or group had the right to oppose the royal will. No compromises with existing institutions were either necessary or desirable. In order to enforce his decrees, armies of bureaucrats were needed to ensure that his laws were obeyed. It was this inflexible refusal to accept any compromise or opposition to his reforms which distinguishes Joseph from the other Enlightened Despots. Joseph was the only one who actually took the theories of the monarch enjoying total power to their logical conclusion.

The third factor influencing his ideas was Austria's own history. Many of Joseph's most famous reforms, including those in government and education, were in many ways no more than logical extensions of Maria Theresa's earlier efforts. His reforms owed more to the pioneering reforms of his mother than he liked to admit.

3 Joseph as Co-ruler

Maria Theresa, who had been given no preparation at all for her responsibilities by her father, was determined that her son should gain experience and responsibility in government whilst she was still on the throne. Joseph started to attend meetings of the Council from 1760, but was not given any specific responsibilities until the death of his father, the ineffective Francis of Lorraine, in 1765. He succeeded his father as Holy Roman Emperor, and was also proclaimed joint ruler of the

Austrian Empire with his mother. These appeared to be significant responsibilities, but in practice Joseph found they only gave an illusion of power. Maria Theresa still expected to have the last word in all decisions affecting Austria.

* Joseph was able to make a start in reducing the power of the Roman Catholic Church despite the opposition of his mother. In this area he had the strong support of Kaunitz who, like Joseph, had been influenced by the *philosophes'* writings attacking Church wealth and power. In 1769 Joseph and Kaunitz produced a document calling for a wholesale transformation of Austria's religious policies. They called for state control over Church lands and education, and a reduction in Church wealth. Despite Maria Theresa's support for the Roman Catholic Church, the combined forces of Joseph and Kaunitz made it possible for a large proportion of this programme to be implemented. The expulsion of the Jesuits from Austrian lands in 1773 demonstrated Joseph's increasing influence over religious affairs, as Maria Theresa was known to have particular sympathy for the Order, having been educated by them. However, although Austria had moved a long way towards reducing the power of the Church before 1780, Joseph was not satisfied. No progress at all had been made towards establishing religious toleration, and the Catholic Church still enjoyed immense wealth and privilege.

* Joseph's influence over foreign policy became increasingly evident after 1765. Austrian participation in the First Partition of Poland in 1772 was virtually forced on Maria Theresa by Joseph and Kaunitz. Maria Theresa, who had herself been the victim of unprovoked aggression in 1740, had no wish to copy Frederick by attacking a defenceless neighbour. To make things worse, partition meant despoiling a fellow Catholic state and further strengthened her old enemy, Prussia. These objections were not enough to answer Joseph's arguments that Polish land would be good compensation for the loss of Silesia.

Joseph felt that the partition, in which Austria gained the province of Galicia, was a triumph for his diplomacy and that he had restored Austria's power in central Europe, but his other forays into foreign policy in these early years were less successful. He persuaded his mother, cautious as ever, to challenge Prussia once more in Germany by making an issue of the Bavarian Succession in 1778. The war that followed was a great disappointment to Joseph. Commanding part of the army in person, he was unable to get to grips with the Prussian army. There was so little fighting and so much foraging that the war became known as 'The Potato War'. France refused to help its nominal ally and Russia threatened to intervene. A treaty was signed at Teschen in 1779 in which Austria got only a tiny piece of land – some 34 square miles – instead of the whole of Bavaria. Once again Frederick had outmanoeuvred the Austrians.

Joseph had been personally humiliated in the area monarchs were most sensitive about – military glory and diplomacy. The result was an unfortunate determination to obtain revenge. In the long run this led to the irresponsible and aggressive foreign policy of the 1780s which was a major cause of Joseph's failure.

* However it was the peasant problem which caused the sharpest disagreements between Joseph and Maria Theresa. Joseph favoured the total abolition of serfdom, but this was firmly rejected by the cautious Maria Theresa. A particular problem was posed by the serfs of Bohemia. The province had suffered from repeated invasions by Prussia and France between 1740 and 1763 and was dominated by a particularly oppressive group of nobles. A series of bad harvests and epidemics meant that by 1770 the Bohemian serfs faced starvation. What would the government do?

Joseph visited Bohemia in 1771 and was appalled by what he found. He noted that famine was the result rather than the cause of the peasants' problem. The problem was serfdom itself. He demanded a drastic reduction in the *robot* (the unpaid work serfs undertook for their masters) and the seizure of Church wealth to pay for the establishment of schools and almshouses. The Council of State debated the problem at length and referred it to the Bohemian Estates. The Estates, being controlled by the nobles, protested against the ourageous suggestion that central government should intervene in local affairs. By 1774 the desperate peasants were in revolt against their masters.

Joseph felt that he had to act. In 1775 he decreed an Urbarial Law which for the first time laid down the maximum *robot* a serf could be required to undertake. It was to be three days a week for twelve hours a day in summer, eight hours a day in winter. This Law, well short of the total abolition Joseph favoured, was simply ignored by the nobles who continued to demand more *robot*. The peasant revolt spread throughout Bohemia.

Now Joseph had to make a painful decision. He could have supported the peasants, arguing that the revolt was the result of the selfishness of the nobles. However, this would have meant condoning rebellion and facing the strong opposition of both the nobles and his mother. They blamed the Urbarial Law for the peasant revolt because it had given the peasants fantasies about freedom. They demanded that Joseph suppress the revolt and cancel the Law. With great reluctance Joseph ordered the army to crush the peasant revolt.

The affair of the Bohemian peasants was very significant. It caused a real breach between Maria Theresa and Joseph, and illustrates their fundamentally different approaches to government. Maria Theresa put the blame on a reforming law, Joseph on the government's failure to enforce that law. The revolt only confirmed both prejudices and seemed to prove to both that they were in the right. It caused great bitterness amongst the peasants who felt they had been made promises by an emperor who had then betrayed them. Above all it forced Joseph for the first time to choose between his aims: which came first – caring for the people or protecting the state? When he had to choose between being enlightened or being despotic, he chose the latter. Without a strong state to start with, no reforms were possible, so the continued existence of the state had to come first.

It was not the last time Joseph would be forced to make such a choice between his reforms and the preservation of the Habsburg Empire. He would make the same choice again, and by so doing revealed which of his aims was the most important to him.

4 Reforms in Government

'Since I have ascended the throne and wear the first diadem in the world, I have made Philosophy the legislator of my Empire'. These were the words Joseph used to sum up his aims as Austrian Emperor soon after he ascended the throne in 1780. Of all the Enlightened Despots, Joseph had the clearest plans for his state and was the most single-minded in pursuing them. Amongst the most important of these was his vision of the efficient, humane state. He wanted his empire to be a well-organised power which controlled Germany, and where all its subjects were protected by the benevolent Emperor. This could only be achieved if the power of vested interests, particularly the nobles and Church, was destroyed.

Joseph's vision needed a centralised and well-run system of government to enforce the new laws. However, the Austrian government, despite some reforms by Maria Theresa, was itself appallingly inefficient by Joseph's standards. Instead of the single centralised system which Joseph wanted, and which seemed to operate in Prussia, the new Emperor found a bewildering variety. Only in Austria and Bohemia was there any direct rule by the Crown, and even here local Diets continued to function with limited powers. The further one went from Vienna the less control the Emperor exercised. In Hungary, Maria Theresa had been forced to confirm the existing system of government in return for Hungarian assistance against Frederick the Great in 1741. Here the nobles controlled everything. A central Diet met only rarely, but local county assemblies ran administration, justice, education, tax-collection and the Church. The taxes they contributed to the Habsburg Empire were insignificant compared to Hungary's size and wealth. The peasants worked under an oppressive system of serfdom, and justice was arbitrary. The execution of 115 gypsies in one batch in 1782 on trumped up charges by one magistrate was not untypical of the judicial abuses in this province. Hungary was, in effect, self-governing under the control of the nobles, with only nominal allegiance to the Habsburgs. Maria Theresa had made no attempt to remove Hungary's special privileges or to integrate it into the Empire. Joseph regarded the reform of government in Hungary as one of his highest priorities.

The Austrian Netherlands also presented a serious problem. Geographically distant from Austria, the different provinces enjoyed a complicated and varied system of government dating back to medieval times. Each province had its own system of Estates, and in a few the Estates had retained the specific rights to approve legislation and to vote taxes. Once again it was the nobles who dominated the Estates, and with it justice and the Church. Despite this the Netherlands were much less of a problem than Hungary. There was no tradition of independence or defiance of authority; the people knew that they needed Austrian protection against French aggression; there was no serfdom and the economy was well developed. Above all, the Netherlands paid more than its fair share of taxes. Under the circumstances Maria Theresa had seen no reason to spoil a mutually profitable arrangement with the Belgian nobles, and in one of her last letters when she knew she was dying, urged Joseph to make no changes. 'The peoples of these provinces' she wrote 'hold to their traditional prejudices – perhaps ridiculous; but since they are obedient and faithful, and pay more taxes than our German provinces, what more can we ask of them?'. Joseph paid a visit to the Netherlands in 1781 – the first ruler for 200 years to actually visit the province – and quickly decided that there was a great deal more that could be asked. He was appalled at the inefficient system of government, the way the same nobles combined administrative, judicial and clerical posts, the wealth of the Church and its persecutions of Protestants, and the depressed state of the peasants. Here too reform was needed.

Joseph felt that administrative reform was essential. He wanted to replace his multi-national Empire of various systems of government with a single unitary state. Such a reform would itself break the power of the nobles, and would then allow other essential reforms in the Empire. To Joseph the solution was simple. He would simply abolish the old systems of government and introduce new and improved ones.

* The first step was to tighten royal control over central government in Vienna. Joseph combined a number of existing administrative bodies into a single Chancellery which supervised all areas of government except foreign policy, justice, and the army. The Emperor chaired its meetings and issued orders to the ministers. There was no Council of Ministers. In this way Joseph was able to act as his own Prime Minister. Although he retained most of Maria Theresa's ministers in their existing posts, only Kaunitz retained any ability to act independently as Joseph often deferred to his greater experience in foreign affairs. In return Kaunitz did not interfere in domestic policy. By contrast, ministers with responsibility for domestic affairs were treated as servants, and Joseph frequently issued decrees without consulting them. His whole style of government, along with its structure, was similar to that of Frederick.

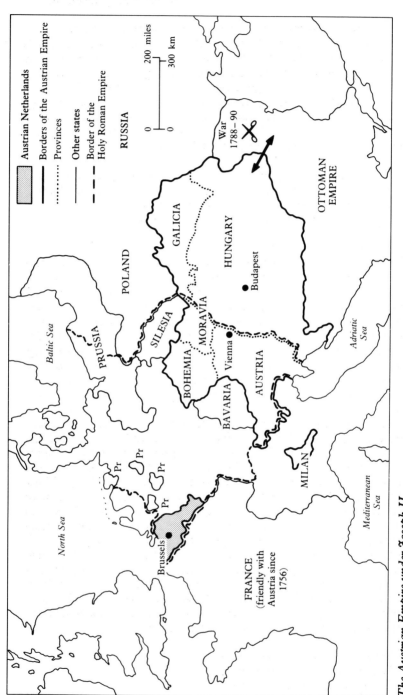

The Austrian Empire under Joseph II

* Joseph's most important soldiers in his war against the old system were his civil servants. He recognised their crucial role by greatly extending their influence throughout his Empire and by giving them job security with very generous pensions for long service. In every other respect his actions, although designed to improve their efficiency, in practice often had the opposite effect. They were required to work longer hours and in many cases had pay cuts. They were constantly reminded of the necessity for hard work and total commitment. In one decree, typical of many, Joseph reminds them that

1 They must not act purely as copyists, nor devote their backsides to sitting and their hands to signing, but must sacrifice their souls, their reason, their wills and their whole strength to their work without considering the hours they are working.

Joseph found it was not easy to create an army of miniature Josephs from his civil servants. Old habits died hard, and often civil servants identified themselves with the areas they worked in rather than the wishes of the Emperor. Joseph, like Frederick, spent many weeks each year personally supervising his civil servants. He would attend meetings and take notes, turn up unexpectedly to inspect papers, and would dismiss civil servants he found not working hard enough. The civil servants were required to spy on each other and to report any failings direct to the Emperor. In addition a secret police force was established whose primary function was to check up on civil servants. Senior officials had to submit detailed questionnaires twice a year on each of their juniors.

The civil servants were simply overwhelmed by the large number of decrees they were expected to enforce. It is doubtful whether any other ruler in history has passed as many laws as Joseph did in his ten years as Emperor. He issued a total of 17000 decrees of which 6000 were new laws – an average of about two new laws every day of his reign. These ranged from far-reaching laws such as those abolishing serfdom or establishing religious toleration, to an enormous number of decrees on trivial subjects. Many of these, such as the law banning people from drinking dirty water, were unenforceable in practice. Mounting evidence that his laws were being ignored by his own civil servants seemed only to prove to Joseph how inefficient they were. Accordingly in 1784 he created a new post of District Commissioner for each province, whose job it was to check whether laws were being enforced. The list of their precise responsibilities is revealing about what Joseph expected to see happening in his realm: They were to observe:

1 Whether the census registers were kept.
  Whether the houses were numbered.
  The condition of the buildings.

Whether the people were industrious or lazy; well-to-do or poor,
5 and why.
Whether the conscription books were kept in order.
Whether the barracks were habitable.
How many men could be quartered amongst the citizens.
Whether the army behaved properly to the civilians.
10 Whether the Toleration Edicts were being observed.
Whether there was any superstition.
Whether the clergy were respected.
Whether divine services were properly carried out, and whether
the churches were in good condition.
15 Whether the priests delivered indiscreet sermons.
Whether anyone cared for orphans, foundlings and homeless
children.
Whether anything was being done for the blind, deaf and crippled
children.
20 The condition of the schools.
Whether there were any clowns or jugglers on the land.
Whether the laws against drunkenness were being carried out.
Whether more prisons and workhouses wre needed.
Whether the laws were being carried out.
25 Whether the roads were cleaned.
Whether there were sufficient precautions in the sale of poisons.
Whether the sale of contraceptives was prohibited.
Whether the penances and dishonouring punishments of unfor-
tunate girls were abolished, and whether there were institutions
30 for the saving of such girls.

This shows the vast range of subjects that interested him, from the
important to the trivial. Yet for all the apparently exhaustive and
detailed checking that this list implies, it is very doubtful whether it
helped improve the efficiency of the civil service as he hoped. Far from
spurring the civil service into carrying out its responsibilities, the
evidence suggests that Joseph had created a new branch of the civil
service, as incapable of carrying out its wide-ranging task as the people
it was supposed to be supervising.

After reforming central government and the civil service, the next
step was to create a unified system of local government. In Austria and
Bohemia, the provinces already most under government control, this
was achieved relatively easily. The number of *gubernia* (provinces) was
reduced to six, each run by a committee of civil servants and a governor
appointed by Joseph. The local Estates were not abolished, but had
their few remaining powers further pruned.

★ It was not long before Joseph was extending his administrative
reforms to the much more sensitive areas of Hungary and the Nether-

lands. He was well aware of the controversy this would arouse, but believed firm action was all that was required. As early as 1765 he summarised his views on how to deal with opposition in a famous letter:

1 Great things have to be accomplished at a stroke. All change arouses controversy. The best way of going about things is to inform the public of one's intentions at once and, having made one's decision, to listen to no contrary opinion and resolutely
5 carry it out.

His first step was to refuse to be crowned at Budapest – this would have meant taking the same oath as his mother in order to maintain the Hungarian nobles' privileges. He began introducing German civil servants into key positions in Hungary. The Diet was not summoned in the hope that this would prevent any focus of opposition. In 1784, in one of his most radical reforms, Joseph decreed that German should be the official language of the Empire. All official documents were to be written in German, and anyone seeking government office must speak German. German teaching was introduced into schools throughout the Empire to facilitate this. This decree aroused immense opposition, particularly in Hungary and the Netherlands. It seemed to be an attack on their culture and civilisation, and an attempt to turn the whole Empire into a single German state. Despite the apparently laudable aim of simplifying and unifying the system of government in the Empire, this was one of Joseph's least realistic laws. Far from gradually Germanising the educated élite in his Empire, it only increased their awareness of their own cultural and linguistic identity.

In Hungary, Joseph continued the work of reform. He reogranised local government, dividing Hungary into provinces run by German civil servants. He enforced his reforms in education, justice and religion. Finally he proposed to start taxing the nobles. Unfortunately it was at this stage – 1788 – that he was obliged to ask the Hungarian nobles for soldiers, money and supplies for his impending war with Turkey. He refused to summon the Diet, and instead summoned the district assemblies. These meetings gave the nobles the opportunity to refuse the supplies and to demand the dismantling of the reforms. It was a symptom of the desperation of the nobles that some contacted the new King of Prussia, Frederick William II, to seek his help in overthrowing Joseph.

* Joseph was now experiencing the basic paradox of Enlightened Despotism; a ruler could only be despotic if he ruled with the co-operation of the nobles, but if he relied on their co-operation enlightened reforms could not take place.

Joseph faced similar problems in the Netherlands. Again he introduced a series of unpopular measures, including the language decree and his reforms of justice and the Church. In 1787 he undertook a sweeping reform of the administration. The old Estates, though not abolished, lost all their powers. The country was divided into provinces, each administered by civil servants and led by an official called the *Intendant*. Joseph assumed that the people would soon realise how much better off they were under this more efficient and paternalistic system. The nobles who stood to lose the most, protested at the removal of their privileges, and they showed some skill in enlisting the support of the peasants and posing as defenders of freedom against a foreign autocrat. Joseph's foreign adventures helped ruin his reforms since, with his army bogged down in Turkey in 1788, he had to watch helplessly from afar whilst the Belgian rebels defeated his small garrisons and obliged the Viceroy, his sister Marie Christine, to cancel the reforms.

In the end Joseph's attempts to impose administrative uniformity on his Empire enjoyed some success in Austria itself, but failed in Hungary and the Netherlands. Joseph, of course, never doubted that these reforms were necessary and desirable, both for his subjects and for himself. He was always surprised when people objected to his plans, particularly when they resisted reforms that would create a more efficient and fair government for the vast majority. He found it particularly ironic that his people were rebelling *against* reforms he was trying to introduce at the same time as the French were rebelling *for* the same sort of reforms.

Joseph's admirers have pointed out that resistance to reform was not led by patriots indignant at foreign takeover of their lands and customs, but by a small number of powerful and selfish nobles struggling to prevent their wealth and privileges being shared out more fairly. Against this, it can be pointed out that it was not the reforms as such that people objected to, but the tyrannical and arbitrary way in which they were introduced, riding roughshod over traditions, customs and culture. Joseph had a vision of a uniform society ruled from above, not unlike many twentieth-century dictatorships. It was the same Joseph who stated that his only aim 'was to make his people happy' who extended the role of the secret police to one of spying on anyone who criticised him, and who ensured that the secret police were outside the jurisdiction of the courts. Joseph may have had humanitarian aims for his new system of government, but the methods he used were those of a dictator and would have been easy for future leaders to abuse. Selfish the nobles may have been in resisting Joseph's administrative reforms, but the verdict of history may well be that they were right to do so.

5 Religion

Joseph had mixed motives for wanting to reform religion. In common with Frederick and Catherine he saw the practical advantages to the state of religious toleration. Such a policy turned despised and persecuted minorities into useful citizens and avoided wasteful and divisive conflicts within a state between rival religions. Joseph was well aware, for example, that the citizens of Silesia had welcomed their takeover by Prussia as the majority of them had been Protestants persecuted by the Austrian government. Religious toleration would also enable him to encourage immigrants of any religion into his lands.

There were practical reasons also for wishing to destroy the power of the Church. The Church owned immense lands and wealth which, Joseph thought, could be more usefully employed by the state. By its control over people's loyalties and its own obedience to the Pope, it represented an alternative centre of power to that of the state. It still had wide-ranging authority, controlling education, welfare, and censorship, and Joseph felt it wasted people's time through an excessive number of saints days.

* These practical reasons for favouring a radical policy towards religion were matched by genuinely enlightened ones. Joseph felt strongly that religious toleration was an essential part of the humane state he was trying to build. What was unusual about Joseph was that he saw himself as a loyal member of the Church whose power he wished to attack. He saw himself as removing what was bad from the Church in order to turn it into a better Church. Some of his reforms, far from trying to destroy the Church, were designed to make it more accessible to people. Above all he wished to remove the superstition from religion. He wrote that 'It is necessary to remove certain things out of religion which never did belong to it. As I myself detest superstitions, I will free my people from them'.

The Edict of Toleration for Protestants (1781) was one of his earliest reforms. It granted Protestants full equality under the law and the right to equal education and to enter the professions, but it only allowed them the right to worship in private. This meant they could worship freely in their own homes, but could not build churches. As a result, this Edict, although a huge step forward from the persecution which they had endured from Maria Theresa, did not give Protestants full equality. They did not yet have the rights enjoyed by minority religions in Russia or Prussia. Nevertheless, the ending of persecution did lead to a significant increase in the number of declared Protestants in the Empire to around 150 000. This increase came as something of a disappointment to Joseph, who seems to have expected that their numbers would decline. However, the Edict remains one of his most successful laws.

Joseph followed this by granting a similar Edict of Toleration for Jews in 1782. This was a far more controversial step. Many states now allowed Jews a grudging equality, but not even in Prussia or Russia were their rights protected by law. In these otherwise most tolerant of states, they were only protected by custom and the goodwill of the monarch. Joseph's grant of toleration was therefore the first such law in Europe, and a major step forward in the history of European Jewry.

Once again the 1782 Edict was a cautious document. Jews were given equality under the law, allowed to enter the professions and to go to university. There were given the right of private worship and no longer had to wear their distinctive clothes or pay their special taxes, but were not permitted to build synagogues. However, a reading of the Edict reveals some interesting motives for the law and suggests that Joseph himself was not immune to some of the popular misconceptions about Jews.

1 In order to make the Jews more useful, the discrimination in relation to their clothing is abolished. The obligation to wear yellow armbands is abolished.
  Within two years the Jews must abandon their own language.
5 From now on all contracts . . . [and other documents] . . . whether of a legal nature or not, must be drawn up in German, Jews may only use their own language during religious services.
  Jews may only engage in agriculture in areas already settled by them, and the land may only be leased [that is, Jews could rent,
10 but not buy, land].
  To prevent Jews suffering, the authorities must instruct the subjects that Jews are like other humans and there must be an end to prejudice . . . On the other hand, Jews are warned not to indulge in swindling.

Joseph also encouraged Jewish children to attend state schools rather than their own schools, and made Jews liable for conscription. Austria was, in fact, the first state to conscript Jews.

The Edict aroused immense opposition from the Church. It was also disliked by many of the Jewish leaders, who feared that the Jews would lose their separate identity and become assimilated into the Christian community. There was particular resentment at the notion of conscripting young Jewish men into the army. But the Jewish community of around 400 000 benefited from the reform in the long run. Many now moved to Vienna and entered the professions and industry. Not only did they contribute significantly to the Austrian economy in the nineteenth century, they were also loyal to the Habsburg monarchy. This Edict was one of Joseph's longest-lasting reforms. It was also one of his most unpopular, even amongst the people it was supposed to help.

  * These decrees were only part of Joseph's approach to religion. Having given legal protection to his religious minorities, he now turned to the reform of the Roman Catholic Church. His reform of the Church amounted to a revolution. Censorship was removed from Church control and was virtually abolished. The result was that for a few years Austria had the freeest press in Europe. Works by the *philosophes* were now freely available, as were books attacking the Roman Catholic

Church. Joseph had about 700 monasteries closed – about one third of the total. The rest were only allowed to continue if they did useful work, such as running schools. The wealth and land seized from the closed monasteries was immense – some 60 million guilders, equivalent to a year's income from taxation. The money was transferred for useful purposes, including the building of schools, which were now removed from Church control.

Other reforms replaced papal control over the Church by state control. Amongst the most important of these was the abolition of tithes (the money which peasants paid each year to the priest), and their replacement by salaries paid by the state. Priests were now civil servants, and expected to preach those virtues which Joseph felt were important – loyalty, obedience and hard work, rather than merely preparing people for heaven.

Joseph's actions appalled the Catholic hierarchy but were not, despite their fears, designed to destroy the Church. On the contrary, he wanted to see the Church strengthened, and he passed a number of laws designed to increase the number of churches and the pay of priests. Large numbers of new churches were built during his reign, including more than 1000 in Hungary alone. These were not the actions of a ruler trying to destroy the Church, but were designed to create a new type of Church with the same aims as his own. In Joseph's new Austria, the priest would stand with the civil servant as another soldier in his war to establish the humane, efficient state.

Such small comforts as the increased number of churches were hardly likely to reassure the Pope, who saw only that his most important Church outside Spain and Italy was being taken away from him. So worried was Pope Pius VI that he decided to visit Joseph and plead with him to cease his attacks on the Church. The Pope's desperation is indicated by the fact that no Pope had visited Austria since 1414. The visit was both a success and a failure. Everywhere the Pope travelled he was greeted by enormous, enthusiastic crowds – an indication of the anger Joseph's reforms were arousing amongst ordinary people. From that point of view the Pope could be well satisfied with the trip. However, he was unable to persuade Joseph to modify a single law. Joseph, anxious to avoid a total breach with Rome, was polite but non-committal. Kaunitz, who strongly supported Joseph's reforms of the Church, openly humiliated the Pope with such petty gestures as receiving him wearing a dressing gown. In the event the Pope returned to Rome having achieved nothing. This humiliation of the figure widely regarded as the foremost enemy of the Enlightenment in Europe, led Joseph to receive the congratulations of his fellow Enlightened Despots, Frederick and Catherine. In many ways the Pope's visit to Vienna represents the low point of the Papacy in the eighteenth century.

Had Joseph restricted his reforms, it is possible that the Pope would never have received any popular demonstrations of support during his visit. The increased numbers of churches and the priests' improved pay pleased most people, while the closing of the monasteries and other reforms were largely unopposed since they affected relatively few people. It was Joseph's interference in Church ritual which led to ordinary people opposing all his reforms. Joseph felt strongly that superstition should be removed from religion, not realising that it was precisely this feature of their Church which was the most important to many ordinary people.

Joseph banned 'unnecessary' church decorations such as candles over gravestones. He ordered all relics to be thrown out. People were not to pay to have clothes put on statues of the Virgin Mary, nor were they to wear lucky charms, kiss pictures or statues. Rules were made about church services and their length. Hymns were to be sung in German, not Latin, and there were rules about the sort of music that could be played. Pilgrimages and processions were banned. People were no longer to kneel in the street when the Host was carried by. There were even rules about the length of candles. Most extraordinary of all was Joseph's attempt to ban coffins in 1784. Instead, the dead were to be buried in sacks. He was only trying to save the peasants unnecessary expense at funerals, but it resulted in such outrage and protest that Joseph had to quickly abandon the idea – one of the few times he withdrew a reform in the face of public protest. His lack of sensitivity to the peasants' attachment to their old superstitions and rituals is surprising for a ruler who was so well-travelled and so careful to find out what ordinary people thought.

Joseph's religious reforms are amongst his most important and most controversial. Most of them did in fact survive him, but they aroused such hostility from the ordinary people that no other reforms he introduced could persuade them to give him their support. Not even when he abolished serfdom.

6 Serfdom

Joseph made it clear through his actions in Bohemia in the 1770s that he favoured the total abolition of serfdom. The institution, which was widespread throughout most of the Habsburg Empire, had been condemned by the *philosophes*, and stood in the way of the creation of his ideal state. Serfdom both hindered the development of agriculture and involved the exploitation of one group of people by another.

In 1781 Joseph issued his decree which announced the abolition of serfdom.

> Serfdom is abolished entirely. In its place a moderate form of subjection is introduced.
>
> 1.   Every subject is entitled to marry . . . there is no charge.

2.   Every subject is free to leave his lord's estate and to seek employment or to settle elsewhere. But those subjects who leave their lords must obtain a certificate to prove that their old lord has released them.
3.   Subjects can learn trades and professions without needing special papers.
4.   No subject is obliged to perform domestic service for his lord.

In the same year other decrees enabled peasants to become landowners and restricted the nobles' right to punish their peasants. The peasants were given the right to appeal against any sentence to a state court using the services of the Peasants' Advocate, a lawyer whose job was specifically to protect the legal rights of serfs. The appeal and the services of the lawyer were free of charge. These were impressive reforms although they did not, in fact, amount to the total abolition of serfdom, since the peasants who remained on the land still had to perform *Robot* (unpaid work) for their Lord.

During the next few years Joseph abolished the remnants of serfdom on the lands he controlled – those owned by the Church and the Crown. The peasants were sold land cheaply and encouraged to build up their holdings by buying extra land from other peasants. Joseph seems to have hoped that his 1781 laws, and the example he set on his own lands, might induce nobles to voluntarily release serfs from their obligations. Few responded, and Joseph realised he would have to pass further laws if he wished to see serfdom eliminated. It was at this point that he decided to combine the final abolition of serfdom with a reform of the tax system. In 1785 he established a commission to recommend changes to the tax system. As a result of its work he felt able to proceed in 1789 to the most far-reaching reform he ever attempted – the Tax and Agrarian Law.

* Hidden behind this innocuous title was his most revolutionary decree. In it he abolished all existing taxes, feudal dues, tithes and the *robot*. Instead there was to be one land tax based on the amount of land owned by the peasant. The tax was not to exceed 30 per cent of the peasant's annual income. The nobles were horrified by the new law. While it was true that they would still receive some money from the peasants, this was insignificant compared to the loss of the dues they used to receive and the value of the serf labour. The nobles claimed that they now faced bankruptcy. Although in the first instance the law only applied to around 20 per cent of their serfs, these were their most productive labourers and Joseph had made it clear that the Law would be quickly extended to all peasants.

It may appear that the Tax and Agrarian Law should have been universally welcomed by the peasants, but it was not. There were several reasons for this. The most important was that it only applied in the first instance to those peasants who already paid more than two guilders a year in tax. The rest would continue to pay feudal dues and do *robot* for the time being. There was great resentment amongst the poorer peasants, who had been led to believe that *robot* would be abolished for all. Even the wealthier peasants who did stand to benefit had little goodwill left for their Emperor. Joseph had antagonised them already through his religious reforms and the imposition of a much stricter system of conscription. Now he told them that they must change their traditional method of farming and that, in return for the land, they must put fences round their fields and breed horses.

The timing of the Law was unfortunate. It was introduced in November 1789 at a time when *ancien régimes* all over Europe were watching with horror the introduction of radical reforms in France, and the violence which was taking place as a result. When the nobles refused to accept the Law, Joseph could not send his army in to impose it since troops were at that time bogged down in an unwinnable war against Turkey. The frustrated peasants rose up in revolt. Joseph found himself with the same dilemma he had faced in Bohemia in the 1770s, and he reacted in the same way. Early in 1790 he suspended the new Law and ordered the army to crush the peasant revolt. The peasants now had to wait until 1848 for serfdom to be abolished. One of Joseph's most important and ambitious reforms had ended in total failure.

* Why was this reform so unsuccessful? As we have seen, Joseph was unlucky in his timing and had been unwise to make promises to the peasants which he could not, in fact, fulfil. However, the crucial factor in the Law's failure was neither of these issues. His reform failed because of the determined opposition of the nobles. That it was possible to abolish serfdom on noble lands without arousing too much antagonism was demonstrated in Prussia in the 1790s and Russia in 1861. In both these cases the nobles were offered financial or other compensation. What is striking about Joseph's reforms is that he resolutely refused to offer the nobles any compensation for their loss of land and workers. One of his motives in introducing this reform was not just to help the peasants, but to break the power and wealth of the nobles, who he perceived as his bitterest enemies. When the nobles complained that Joseph was trying to bankrupt them, they had discerned his motives exactly. Under the circumstances their resistance to the law was inevitable.

Joseph's failure to abolish serfdom underlines the difficulty any ruler faces when trying to reform an outdated social system from above. It is also an example of the problems which faced an eighteenth-century monarch trying to put the fine theories of the writers into practice. Frederick and Catherine preferred not to risk abolishing serfdom, and instead played safe by supporting the privileges of the nobility. The example of Joseph II suggests that they were probably wise.

7 Social Reform

Joseph's enlightenment emerges most strongly in his social reforms, an aspect of his rule which has sometimes been neglected by historians. Before 1780 Austria, like other European states, had no government-funded welfare agencies. Hospitals and schools were the responsibility of the Church, and as a result provision was limited. There was virtually no provision for the old or disabled, while lunatics were usually confined in prisons and treated with great harshness. In this respect Austria was no better and no worse than any other European state.

Joseph established the most comprehensive welfare system in Europe. In this respect he went much further than any of the other Enlightened Despots, most of whom made only nominal improvements to schools and hospitals. Although the *philosophes* argued that the enlightened monarch had a responsibility towards its weaker subjects, none in fact advocated a system as expensive and wide-ranging as that introduced by Joseph. It is the one example of an Enlightened Despot going further than the most radical suggestion of a writer.

He financed his programme largely from money obtained from the dissolution of the monasteries. Orphanages, founding homes (for illegitimate children), hospitals, maternity facilities, medical colleges and institutions for unmarried mothers, the blind, the deaf and crippled children were all established in the 1780s. So too were the first lunatic asylums, in which the patients were to be treated with kindness instead of brutality. By 1785 Vienna General Hospital, the country's largest, had 2000 beds. There were charges for these facilities, but the poor, who were the largest users, paid nothing. Although not as complete as a twentieth-century welfare state, Joseph's provision was the most effective of any state in Europe, and would not be improved in any other country for another century.

Not even Joseph expected to turn a blind crippled lunatic into a soldier or farmer by providing him with an institution. His expensive social reforms show that he had genuine and strongly held humanitarian principles which contrast with the cynicism of Frederick and Catherine. While they wrote letters to Voltaire, Joseph was putting principles into practice.

8 Education

Joseph was opposed to the traditional concept of education – schools organised by the Church with priests acting as schoolmasters. He wished to establish a system of state schools where children would be trained for their future work. The ablest would become civil servants, the other boys farmers or soldiers, while the girls would be taught to become good housewives. His education reforms were geared towards this social engineering.

Schooling was made compulsory for all children of primary age. This was enforced through inspections and fines for parents who did not send their children to school. A new generation of secular school-teachers was attracted by generous salaries. A state-run publishing firm provided textbooks, which were given free to poor children. Primary schools taught basic skills, and the teaching was done in the local language rather than Latin. Joseph was also unusual in making specific provision for state schooling for girls. They were to be given separate schools where possible in which they were mainly taught domestic skills.

Inevitably there was resistance to compulsory schooling. Protestants and Jews were particularly fearful of sending their children to state schools where they would lose their identity, and peasants traditionally wanted their children to start work as soon as possible. In all, around 210000 out of 730000 children of primary age seem to have attended school. This 30 per cent attendance rate clearly indicates that schools were less compulsory than Joseph wished, yet by any standards it was an impressive achievement. Austria had one of the highest literacy rates in Europe and had the highest proportion of children attending schools. Catherine was so impressed with Joseph's reforms that she sent experts to study them as the model for her education reforms in the 1780s.

There was no similar expansion in secondary schools. There were only about 60 schools, called *Gymnasia*. These were fee-paying schools for able boys. The teaching and examinations were in German, and stress was increasingly placed on practical subjects. Here boys were groomed for posts in administration. Joseph's lack of interest in subjects he deemed useless is seen most clearly in his attitude towards the universities. Here he actually reduced the number of universities in the Empire from eight to four with a total of around 5000 students. The number of places for university students was reduced to exactly match the number of openings each year in the civil service. Emphasis was placed on practical subjects such as medicine and Law. By contrast subjects which Joseph felt had no real value, such as foreign languages or music, could no longer be studied. The Church lost its remaining control over the universities, in which lectures were given in German and to which Protestants, Jews, and peasants were now admitted.

Joseph expected a return on his investments. He used the schools to teach children loyalty and obedience, and they were one of his main instruments both for assimilating the children of religious minorities and for spreading the use of German as the language of the Empire. Joseph, for all his admiration of the *philosophes*, had no wish to encourage thinkers in his Empire. He even ended the pension to Mozart, Austria's greatest composer, on the grounds that he was contributing nothing useful to the Empire. Mozart died in poverty because Joseph preferred loyal civil servants to genius. If Joseph's social reforms show him at his humanitarian best, his education reforms show him at his utilitarian worst.

9 Justice

Joseph's legal reforms were impressive and are amongst the few reforms which outlived him. He improved the quality of judges by insisting they pass law examinations – one result was that he was able to remove unqualified nobles who sat as judges in local courts. He did not greatly interfere with the existing system of local courts, but he did add tiers of Appeal Courts, enabling convicted people for the first time to have the opportunity of a fresh trial. Joseph's introduction of legal aid made this process more accessible to the poor. These reforms proved effective in undermining the nobles' control over peasants and in improving the quality of the judges.

* In his new Penal Code (1781) Joseph clearly showed the influence of both Beccaria and his own Law Professor, Martini. He established complete equality under the law as advocated by the *philosophes*. In marked contrast to other countries, nobles now received exactly the same punishments as peasants. There was outrage the first time a noble was sentenced to have his head shaved and to sweep the streets, and when Joseph banned duelling. Joseph followed Beccaria's advice and abolished the death penalty, except for mutiny or desertion. In fact he only allowed one execution during his whole reign. He opposed the death sentence for practical rather than humanitarian reasons. As he wrote to his brother Leopold, 'A death sentence never has the same effect as a lasting heavy punishment; for the first is over and quickly forgotten, but the other is long before the public eye'. Those punished for serious crimes found they would have been better off being hanged, for the ultimate punishment was now flogging followed by hard labour for life, doing such useful work as pulling ships along the Danube. Few prisoners survived more than a few months of this savagery.

The stocks, flogging and branding were retained, but other forms of physical punishment along with torture were abolished. Some activities ceased to be crimes altogether. These included being an unmarried mother or a Christian marrying a Jew. The process of justice was speeded up. An arrested person had to be charged within 24 hours and, in theory at least, brought before a judge within three days. Systems for bail, remand prisons and defence lawyers were established. Joseph's legal reforms were still in force when the Austrian Empire collapsed in 1918. They are amongst his longest-lasting and most successful achievements, yet there were limits to them. Nothing was done to ease the brutalities of prison life, which was a curious omission since Beccaria had stressed the importance of this. But, above all, Joseph established a secret police force which acted outside the laws he had introduced.

Nevertheless there can be no denying his achievement in this field. At a time when an English child could be hanged for stealing five shillings, or a French child burnt at the stake for making fun of a priest, children could not be punished at all in Austria. Joseph's legal system was the fairest and most efficient in Europe. He was the only ruler in Europe to establish equality under the law or to assume innocence until guilt was proved. Beccaria would have been proud of him.

10 Economics

Joseph was familiar both with the ideas of mercantalism – that the state should try to acquire gold, encourage industry and exports and discourage imports – and with those of the Physiocrats, with their stress on freeing trade from government restriction. He saw no reason to have to choose between the two, and his economic policy reflects a mixture of both. It was by no means unsuccessful, but it was seriously undermined by his foreign policy failures.

Joseph abolished all internal customs barriers with the exception of trade from Hungary. He thereby created the largest free trade area in Europe. Economic development was also encouraged by removing nearly all restrictions on industry. He wrote that 'For industry and commerce nothing is more necessary than liberty, nothing more harmful than privileges and monopolies'. He was as good as his word. With a few exceptions (where industries essential for the army continued to enjoy state subsidies), he removed all restrictions and rules from factories. The restrictive powers of the guilds were abolished. In common with other enlightened rulers he offered inducements for factory owners and skilled workers. The latter were exempt from conscription, whilst the former could hope to be ennobled. Joseph ennobled bankers and factory owners, even extending this privilege to Joseph Arnstein, a Jewish banker. In this way Joseph could both reward his most useful citizens and undermine the old nobility.

Immigration of skilled workers from other countries was encouraged by tax exemptions and religious toleration, while the emigration of skilled workers was, rather ineffectively, banned. New roads were built, a postal system was initiated, and money was spent developing the few harbours Austria possessed. An East India Company was started and a few 'factories' (colonies) founded in Africa, India and China. However, the Company went bankrupt in 1787 and Joseph's dream of becoming a colonial power vanished.

Although Joseph's policies were designed to develop industry and encourage foreign trade, these were to some extent negated by the high duties charged on imports – a normal mercantalist policy, but one which encouraged other states to place similar duties on Austrian goods – and his unwise attempt to forbid the use of textile machinery in the hope of protecting the traditional domestic system in Bohemia. Trade figures from this period are incomplete, but it seems that generally his attempts to create a favourable trade balance failed. Although the value of Austrian exports rose from 66 to 87 million guilders a year during his reign, imports rose even more rapidly.

Although there was undoubtedly some industrial development, Austria was still overwhelmingly a rural state. Even in Bohemia, Joseph's most industrialised province, most of her 95 factories would be described as 'workshops' today. Although ten per cent of the population worked in factories in this province, few of them were full-time factory workers. Padover is far too kind to Joseph when he claims that 'He found Austria a feudal country and left her a modern state'. The fact was that, despite all of Joseph's efforts, Bohemia was no substitute for Silesia, the only developed province Austria had.

One result of the improved economy and increased population was a significant increase in tax income from 66 million to 90 million guilders a year. For a time Joseph was able to balance his budget. Although the existing system of taxes seemed to be working well, he was attracted by the Physiocratic idea of a land tax. This, he felt, would not only help the peasants, but would also establish a sound foundation for the state's income. In addition, it would be a fair tax because the amount of land a person owned reflected his wealth; it would hit the noble much harder than the peasant. It would be relatively easy to enforce, provided the government knew how much land everyone owned and provided that changes in the amount of land owned happened only rarely. From 1785 the activities of Joseph's officials assessing how much land everyone owned gave warning to the nobles that they were about to be taxed. They also led to the rumour amongst the serfs that the assessment was going to lead to the total abolition of serfdom. However, when the new tax was introduced in 1789, it was withdrawn within a few weeks due to the protests which greeted its introduction (see page 107).

It is possible to argue that until 1788 Joseph's economic and financial policies were a success. However, all his achievements were jeopardised by his decision in that year to go to war against Turkey. The war proved to be a disaster. Not only was Joseph unable to defeat the Turks, but the war bankrupted the state. When Joseph died, he left his successor a debt of 370 million guilders – equivalent to four years income from taxes. A disastrous defeat in foreign policy and the failure of the new land tax outweighed any modest benefit Joseph's economic and financial policies might have brought to his people.

11 The Last Months

Joseph aimed to integrate all his provinces into a unified empire and to crush the power of the nobles. These were tasks which had been carefully avoided by Maria Theresa. Joseph was confident that, backed by the power of the modern state, opposition from a handful of selfish nobles would quickly crumble. Events were to prove that the nobles in both Hungary and the Netherlands were quite capable of defending their privileges against their reforming monarch.

Starting in 1788, Joseph rapidly lost control over his Empire. There were a number of reasons for this. One factor was his own health, which deteriorated rapidly, leading to his death in February 1790 at the age of 49. Although he tried to retain his grip over his Empire – he was still signing decrees a few hours before his death – there was an inevitable resistance to his reforms when the nobles could see that he would not live much longer. The second factor was the war with Turkey. This was not only disastrously expensive but it also meant that his army was unable to intervene to crush the Belgian and Hungarian nobles. It was not long before they took advantage of this weakness. The years 1788–9 saw economic depression and poor harvests throughout Europe. The depression which helped create the bitter mood in Paris in 1789 also affected the Austrian Empire, disrupting trade and causing food shortages. The result was a series of peasant revolts starting in 1788 with ostensibly difference causes – against Joseph's clerical reforms, against conscription, or for the abolition of serfdom. The nobles demanded that Joseph take firm action against the peasants and that he cease his reforms.

It was in 1789 that the French Revolution began. The nobility saw the Revolution as proof of the disaster which occurred once one made concessions to the people. Events in France also had a direct impact on the neighbouring Austrian Netherlands. Impressed by the example of ordinary people asserting their rights through a States-General against a 'tyrannical' monarch, the nobles in the Netherlands summoned their own Estates and declared their independence as the United States of Belgium. It was Joseph's tragedy that he lived just long enough to be forced to make hard decisions about his reforms, but not long enough to know whether any of his achievements would last. In 1789 he faced the crisis of his reign. If he persisted in his reforms, there seemed a real danger that his Empire would collapse. He had already lost the Netherlands, would almost certainly lose Hungary, and would face revolts in Austria and Bohemia. On the other hand, if he withdrew his reforms it would mean the end of all his dreams.

Joseph chose to sacrifice the reforms. In late 1789 he postponed the introduction of the new land tax and the abolition of *robot*. At the same time he re-imposed strict censorship, increased the activities of the secret police, and ordered the army to crush peasant revolts. In January 1790 he went further. To the Netherlands he offered to cancel all the administrative reforms and restore the traditional system of government to the province. The nobles rejected Joseph's concessions as inadequate. In Hungary he agreed to summon the Diet, and cancelled all the reforms except for religious toleration, the reorganisation of the

Church, and the 1781 decree on serfdom. In short, he restored the old system of government by the nobles.

A few weeks later Joseph died and was succeeded by his brother, Leopold II, a man who shared many of his ideals, but who was much more pragmatic. He had to sacrifice some more of Joseph's reforms, including the abolition of tithes and state control over theological colleges, but was able to win back both the Netherlands and Hungary and retain most of Joseph's remaining reforms through a mixture of firmness and conciliation.

Joseph had no doubt in the end he had totally failed. 'Here lies Joseph II' he ordered to be written on his tomb, 'who failed in everything he attempted'. This was a very harsh judgement to make on himself, although understandable in the apparent chaos of February 1790. In many respects the judgment is unfair. Even the reactionary Francis II (1792–1835) did not cancel the education reforms, the reduction in the power of the Roman Catholic Church, religious toleration, the legal reforms, the almshouses or the hospitals. Other permanent achievements although not ones which one might have expected from an enlightened monarch, were the creation of the secret police and the expansion of the army. Even with the peasants he had not completely failed. Although serfdom was retained, the peasants did now enjoy more legal rights and had easy access to the courts if the nobles abused their powers.

Joseph would have been unimpressed by these achievements. They were precisely the compromises he had always despised. His dream of an efficient, humane state had not been realised. He had wanted to create an absolute monarchy; a state where everyone worked hard and lived under identical rules; where there were no privileged and powerful nobles and clergy, and where government was centralised and administered by German-speaking civil servants who were obedient and loyal. He had wanted a successful state which was feared and respected by others. He had wanted to conquer land. He had wanted to catch up with Prussia. He had wanted his people to be looked after and he had aimed to abolish serfdom. None of these aims were achieved. When he died Austria was in turmoil. Royal power had all but collapsed and the nobles were reasserting themselves. The Netherlands had been lost, and Hungary nearly lost. The people were waiting for him to die, and greeted his death with celebrations – one Bishop even ordered a *Te Deum* as thanksgiving. On hearing that his Emperor was dead, Kaunitz is said to have commented, 'Not before time'. Clearly not even his closest advisers wished their Emperor well.

* What went wrong with Joseph's reforms? It is possible to identify a number of mistakes he made. He was too rash and impatient, eager for instant results. He thought that Prussia had achieved greatness overnight, and sought to copy this example, completely missing the significance of the reign of Frederick William I. As Frederick II put it, 'He took the second step before the first'. If Maria Theresa was too cautious, Joseph was too hasty. He overrated his own power. He believed he could do what he liked as absolute monarch, and did not appreciate that 'absolute' monarchy only worked when the king acted in partnership with the nobles. He did not try to gain support from the peasants, the civil servants, the middle class or the intellectuals, all groups which stood to benefit from his reforms and which might have become his supporters against the nobles and Church. He was too theoretical, issuing decrees which he should have realised would not work or might even be counter-productive. His interference in religious rituals and the attempt to Germanise his people are examples of these. He was unable to distinguish the important from the trivial, and overwhelmed his civil service with decrees. He lacked the ability to compromise – it is revealing just how much of Joseph's work Leopold was able to save with some judicious concessions to the nobles and the Hungarians. This suggests that it was not so much Joseph's aims as his methods which alienated people, and that with a more conciliatory approach he might have achieved far more of his ambitions. His own lack of skill in diplomacy and war were important weaknesses. While they may not appear to be significant in domestic affairs, these failings suggested a lack of skill in an area which both monarchs and peoples saw as crucial to the credibility of a king; they bankrupted his state and destroyed his ability to resist the nobles just when it was needed most. He can also be criticised for his obsession with Prussia.

In later years peasants sometimes put up little memorials in their villages to their 'People's Emperor' who had tried to help them. The Austrian revolutionaries who nearly succeeded in overthrowing the *ancien régime* in 1848 admired Joseph and briefly copied his laws. However, in contrast to either Frederick or Catherine, he had very little influence over the later history of the Austrian Empire. Historians have, on the whole, been critical of Joseph, using him as a good example of how not to rule a country. Of his biographers, only Padover has strongly defended his achievements, stressing the failure of Maria Theresa to modernise her state or Church.

After Joseph's death Austria reverted to a traditional monarchy, where the combination of monarchy and nobility was sufficiently strong to keep the peasants in place. What is surprising is that this multi-national, ramshackle Empire, having rejected Joseph's attempt to modernise and strengthen it, nevertheless survived repeated defeats by Napoleon in 1796, 1800, 1805 and 1809 and retained its position as a Great Power. By contrast the apparently much stronger Prussia, which Joseph had admired, feared and tried to copy, collapsed at once when attacked by Napoleon in 1806. Perhaps Austria had never been as weak as she appeared, and Prussia never as strong.

Joseph was not a complete failure, but it is true that he had achieved

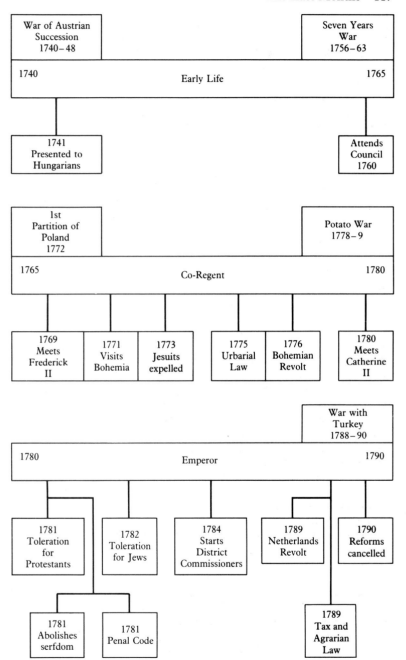

Summary – Joseph II

none of his main aims. There was perhaps one underlying reason for this. He had a vision of an ideal state and tried to impose this model by force on a complex and conservative society. It was a mistake which many later rulers have made, and continue to make today. In the end it was, perhaps, a good thing that he failed.

Making notes on 'Joseph II'

When making notes on Joseph you should remember in each section to look at (i) the problems Joseph faced, (ii) his aims, (iii) the extent to which he was following enlightened theory, and (iv) the extent of his success. Bear in mind, however, that there are different definitions of 'success'.

One way to judge Joseph's success is to ask whether he achieved his aims. Another way is to ask whether his policies strengthened the state or benefited the people. It would, for instance, be perfectly reasonable to maintain that Joseph failed to achieve any of his aims, but was a successful ruler who greatly helped his people. When you have finished making your notes, you should have a clear idea of his successes and failures, and be well on the way to explaining why he was not more successful.

The following headings may help to structure your notes.

1.   Early Life
1.1. Education – the influence of the *philosophes*
1.2. Joseph's attitude towards his empire and his subjects
1.3. His relationship with his mother
1.4. Maria Theresa's reforms
1.5. Assessment of Maria Theresa
2.   Political Philosophy
3.   Joseph as Co-ruler
3.1. Religious policy
3.2. Foreign policy
3.3. The serfs
4.   Reforms in Government
4.1. The government in 1780
4.2. Reforms in central government
4.3. Role of the civil service
4.4. Hungary and the Netherlands – resistance to reform
5.   Religion
5.1. The Edicts of Toleration
5.2. Reform of the Catholic Church
6.   Serfdom

Answering essay questions on 'Joseph II'

Questions on Joseph often focus on one or more of these aspects of his reign: (i) his aims, (ii) his methods, (iii) his achievements, (iv) his failures (particularly when compared to his aims), (v) the reasons for his failures, and (vi) the effects of his policies on the Austrian Empire.
   Carefully read these questions:

1. 'Comment on the view that the policies of Joseph II may have been hasty and sweeping, but were certainly not disastrous.'
2. '"His sincerity was his greatest weakness." How far do you agree with this assessment of Joseph II?'

Both of these questions are clearly of the 'challenging statement' type, which we looked at in the last chapter. You will notice from question 1 that a 'challenging statement' question does not always need an actual quotation.
   The first step in preparing to answer question 1 is to identify the three questions the examiner is asking. What are they? The next step is to work out which aspects of Joseph's reign will need to be covered to answer the questions.
   Design an essay plan for this question. Which examples of Joseph's reforms will you use to decide whether his policies were 'hasty', and which to decide whether they were 'sweeping'? The essay title then broadens out to include the effects of these policies on Austria. Were they in fact 'not disastrous', as the examiner suggests? In order to answer this, will you limit yourself to Joseph's reign, or will you consider what happened after his death?
   You will now be able to try the same approach with question 2. (i) Which aspect, as listed above, is this question asking about? (ii) Which particular cause or reason is identified?
   You will now need to discuss all the other possible causes. Prepare an essay plan. The cause the examiner has named should be discussed

first, but this will only take up perhaps two or three paragraphs. Now list all the other possible causes that you will need to cover. Which cause or causes will you identify in your conclusion as being the most valid one(s)? Is the examiner right in this case?

Remember that you should not be afraid to disagree with the examiner's interpretation, provided that you can offer clear supporting evidence to back up an alternative explanation. In this case, for instance, it should be easy to find alternative explanations which are at least as valid as the one offered by the examiner.

You will now be able to adopt the same approach of identifying the aspect of Joseph's reign, summarising the examiner's opinion, and listing all the other possible answers or factors for the following questions as well.

3. '"His mistake was to believe his own propaganda." Discuss this judgment on the "enlightened" policies of Joseph II.'
4. '"Joseph II was a revolutionary." Discuss.'
5. '"The monarch was never sufficiently absolute to succeed in being enlightened." How does the reign of Joseph II illustrate this weakness of Enlightened Despotism?'
6. '"Here lies a prince who, despite his best intentions, could realise none of his aims." Was Joseph too harsh a judge of his own achievements?'
7. '"Joseph's reign proves that good intentions do not make a good ruler." Do you agree?'
8. '"The nature and strength of the opposition to his policies are powerful testimony to Joseph II's enlightened rule." Discuss.'

Source-based questions on 'Joseph II'

1. The theory and practice of Enlightened Despotism
Read Joseph's statement to his civil servants on page 99, his letter on page 101, and the Instructions to his District Commissioners on pages 99–100. Answer the following questions:
a) Explain what is meant by 'copyists' (page 99 line 1), 'conscription books' (page 100 line 6), and 'penances' (page 100 line 28).
(3 marks)
b) How far do these extracts explain Joseph's own aims and methods? (7 marks)
c) Which aspects of peoples lives was Joseph most interested in finding out about, according to his Instructions to the District Commissioners? (4 marks)
d) Discuss the view that these extracts explain the failure of Joseph to modernise the system of government in his empire. (6 marks)

2 Joseph's reforms

Read the Edict of Toleration for Jews on page 104 and the Decree abolishing serfdom on pages 106–7. Answer the following questions:

a) What reasons does Joseph offer for wanting to abolish serfdom and for granting toleration to the Jews?   (6 marks)

b) What evidence is there from the Edict of Toleration that Joseph shared some of the prejudices against Jews?   (3 marks)

c) The decree on serfdom was titled Edict to Abolish Serfdom. Was this an accurate description of the law? Give reasons for your answer.   (3 marks)

d) Use these sources to comment on the view that Joseph's reforms were always practical rather than idealistic.   (8 marks)

CHAPTER 6

The Minor Enlightened Despots

1 Introduction

None of the rulers described as Enlightened Despots – Frederick II, Catherine II and Joseph II – came close to realising the ideals of the writers of the period, although, as we have seen, some of the policies of each were influenced by the ideas of the Enlightenment. In many ways the most successful and genuinely enlightened of the despots were a handful of the rulers of the minor states of Europe.

In some ways it was much easier for these rulers to put ideals into practice. In most cases the country they ruled was unaffected by the wars of the period. Having neither the wish nor the ability to develop into Great Powers or to conquer land, the rulers were able to concentrate on domestic reform. When kings such as Frederick II were spending up to 80 per cent of their taxes on the army and were involved in frequent wars and invasions, it is not surprising that domestic reform was given a lower priority. Meanwhile, states as far apart and as different as Spain and Sweden had monarchs who experimented with enlightened ideas and practices during the eighteenth century. One of the most successful was the younger brother of Joseph II of Austria.

2 Leopold II: Tuscany 1765–90

Leopold, the younger son of Maria Theresa, was sent to govern the Habsburg province of Tuscany in 1765 when he was just 19 years old. In many ways this was an easy state to rule. It was relatively prosperous, with a strong artistic and cultural tradition. Italy was at this time largely a backwater in European power politics and not once in his 25 years as ruler did Leopold have to worry about a war affecting his country. For the first five years of his rule he had to submit his proposed laws to Maria Theresa for approval, but from 1770 he was given a free hand to run the state as he wished. It may be thought significant that he was given this freedom and power at a much earlier age than Joseph, and was therefore far more experienced as a ruler than his more famous elder brother.

Leopold was well aware of the writings of the *philosophes*, and in particular was strongly influenced by the Physiocrats and by Beccaria, whose *Crime and Punishment* was published in the year Leopold became ruler of Tuscany.

Leopold's attitude towards penal policy was probably the most radical of any ruler at that time. He abolished the use of torture and had the instruments of torture displayed in a museum. While he did not completely abolish the death penalty as Beccaria wished, he did restrict it to parricide (murdering one's father) and *lèse-majesté* (insulting or attacking the ruler of the state). He also abolished secret trials and the confiscation of criminals' property. He greatly restricted the legal rights of nobles, including their much prized hunting rights. In the 1780s he even went as far as to abolish the Inquisition in Tuscany. This institution, which had been set up in most Catholic countries during the sixteenth century, existed to seek out and destroy heretics. In many ways it acted as a state within a state. It accepted anonymous denunciations and was empowered to torture, and in this way could act as a rival to the state's own legal structure. The accused person was not always told who had accused him or what he was accused of. It was an institution which was strongly hostile to the Enlightenment and those who supported it. Yet this same institution enjoyed strong support from ordinary people. With religion as the main focus for people's loyalties before patriotism became a major force, it was easy for the Church to portray the Inquisition as a desirable and necessary institution to suppress such dangerous enemies as the Protestants, Jews, or those who would deny the existence of God entirely.

Leopold gave Tuscany a humane and fair system of laws. His reforms encouraged the Tuscans to take responsibility for administering justice themselves by having trials conducted by local magistrates rather than Austrian officials. He also came close to the ideal proclaimed by the *philosophes* of equality under the law, both by removing the special rights of nobles and by increasing the rights of his ordinary subjects. In general it was an impressive achievement of penal reform, and one clearly influenced by enlightened ideas.

Leopold's economic policies were less radical, but no less successful for that. Francesco Gianni, who acted as his Chief Minister after 1776, introduced a single system of public finance. Previously each of the towns which made up Tuscan had its own system of tax collection and expenditure. As well as simplifying the tax system, Gianni also made it fairer. Tuscany was the first state in Europe in which the taxes people paid were related to their income. Even members of the royal family were liable to pay taxes. The simplification of the tax system enabled Leopold both to reduce taxes and to increase his income. New methods of farming such as crop rotation and the use of fertilisers were encouraged, free trade in grain – always strongly favoured by the Physiocrats – was established in 1767, the remaining serfs were freed and an Academy of Agriculture was started. This adoption of Physiocratic principles earned Leopold the flattery of the *philosophes*. To encourage trade, roads were built. Marshes were drained. The Craft Guilds were abolished in 1770. These medieval institutions had long outlived their usefulness, and now merely served to restrict the growth of trade by allowing only their own members to take part in trade and commerce. With their abolition, anyone could set up as a merchant or a banker. These reforms greatly stimulated the revival of prosperity in the state. By 1790 Tuscany was considered the wealthiest state in Italy, and its main port, Leghorn, developed into the busiest and most important port in southern Europe.

Leopold showed the most originality in his attitude to foreign affairs. He had not the slightest wish for Tuscany to expand its borders. He worked hard to reduce tension in Italy and to cut the size of the armed forces. He actually abolished the Tuscan army, keeping only a police force for Leghorn. The Tuscan navy was sold to Catherine the Great. He tried to ensure that Tuscany was treated as a neutral state – rather like the position that Switzerland has enjoyed for the last 150 years. He was the only ruler of the eighteenth century who argued that wars were not merely unnecessary, but morally unjustifiable. This view actually went further than those put forward by the *philosophes*.

Why did Leopold take this radical line towards foreign policy? No doubt it was partly practical politics – Tuscany was simply too small to ever hope to become a Great Power. But, more importantly, Leopold had no wish to become 'Great'. He was the only example of a pacifist ruler in the eighteenth century.

Until about 1780 Leopold moved cautiously in Tuscany. In his early years he was genuinely anxious to govern with the consent of his people. He was a reserved, modest ruler who neither sought nor expected popularity, but who was able to achieve a broad measure of support for his reforms. This changed in the 1780s when he started to adopt more radical policies, despite the opposition of his people.

Perhaps his most sensational idea was the Charter of 1782. In it he proposed to establish a Consultative Assembly. The existing local assemblies were to send delegates to a central assembly. For the first time the delegates would include representatives of all groups of taxpayers. Any proposed changes to the laws, the tax system, foreign policy or the succession to the throne would require the approval of this assembly, although it would not have the power to propose its own laws. This was a unique move by a ruler to voluntarily hand over some of his power to an elected assembly. It reflected Leopold's feeling that a ruler was answerable to his people and should have clearly defined and limited power. He was, in fact, proposing to turn himself into a constitutional monarch.

On the face of it the Charter of 1782 should be convincing proof that Leopold was a most enlightened ruler. However, the Charter, like Catherine's *Nakaz*, was never actually put into practice. Faced with widespread criticism of the proposal, he felt unable to impose the Charter on his people against their wishes. However, Leopold's other reforms are enough to show that his motives were genuine. He cannot be accused of putting up the proposal merely in order to get the applause of the *philosophes* as Catherine might have done with her *Nakaz*. Yet even had the Charter been put into practice, it would only have been a modest step towards establishing a representative assembly. Leopold's proposed assembly would have been elected indirectly and with only token representation from the middle and lower classes. Its actual powers would have been very limited. The Charter was a major step away from absolutism, but was a long way from democracy.

Leopold turned his attention to the powerful Catholic Church in his last years as ruler of Tuscany. He had been able to cut down the powers of the nobility without difficulty since they had long been in a weaker position in his state than in most others; but the Church retained a great deal of wealth, power and popular support. The decision to abolish the Inquisition had already aroused considerable opposition. He now decided to go further and emulate the religious reforms being undertaken by his brother in Vienna. He started taxing the clergy and introduced major reforms to the structure of the Church. Papal control over the Church was ended, as was the sending of money to Rome. Religious courts lost most of their power and the Church much of its lands. Many monasteries were closed, and the money raised from them was used for public welfare. Leopold was again able to override the objections of these reforms, but found himself facing a well-organised protest campaign when he extended the reforms to areas which directly affected ordinary people. Saints days were reduced, tithes and sanctuary were abolished, and changes made in the way services were conducted. These reforms aroused widespread popular opposition, including a serious riot. At last the embattled nobles and clergy were able to resist Leopold by making common cause with the supersitious peasantry.

Increasingly in his last years Leopold had to rely on an active secret police force to spy on and root out opponents. In earlier years he had governed with consent. By the time he left Tuscany to take over as ruler of Austria after the death of Joseph in 1790, opposition to him was strong and increasing. Had he reigned for much longer he might have had to face the same open opposition as Joseph did in Austria.

In 1790 Leopold left Tuscany to take over the troubled throne of Austria. The chaotic state of the Empire, and the brevity of his reign – he died in 1792 – meant that he had no opportunity to extend reforms to his new state. His years in Austria were dominated by his successful attempt to conciliate the nobles and to regain the Netherlands. He abandoned some of Joseph's most unpopular reforms, but was able to retain some of the most important ones. Even though he was now ruler of a Great Power, he showed the same reluctance to get involved in wars. He had some sympathy for the aims of the French Revolution, and refused to go to war to crush it, despite the fact that his own sister, Queen Marie-Antoinette, was a prisoner in Paris.

Leopold was a genuinely enlightened ruler who wished to govern with the consent of his people. He wanted to establish himself as a constitutional monarch. In a famous letter to his brother Joseph II he explained that a ruler must always be willing to give his subjects a

complete account of the finances and administration; such an account
was 'glorious, useful and just'. The finances were 'a public matter' and
the ruler must only spend money in accordance with the wishes of his
subjects, for the benefit of the state and its people. His task was made
easier by the lack of a strong nobility, the support of some able Tuscan
administrators like Gianni, and the fact that he ruled a small, prosperous state. As Austrian Emperor he was given no opportunity to
introduce reforms, but did show qualities of caution, conciliation and
realism which his more famous brother had noticeably lacked. Writers
such as Voltaire were more impressed with Frederick and Catherine,
yet Leopold had come closer than them to being the ideal Enlightened
Despot.

Unfortunately he moved too fast for his people in Tuscany and
eventually had to resort to despotic methods to impose his will.
Increasingly in his later years he was seen as a foreign ruler with foreign
ideas. Even this most enlightened, able and successful of rulers failed
when faced with the irrational force of religious intolerance.

3 Charles IV: Naples 1734–59

Charles IV of Naples, later to become Charles III of Spain, shares with
Leopold the distinction of acting as ruler of two different states, and of
moving, after a long political apprenticeship ruling a minor state, to
becoming King of a major state.

The Naples that Charles began to rule in 1734 was one of the most
backward states in Europe. The Church and nobles owned most of the
land. Serfdom was still widespread and the condition of the peasants
was abject. Many still lived in mud huts or caves. In many parts of the
country even the rainwater and animal manure belonged to the nobles.
By contrast the Church was immensely wealthy. A total population of
under five million supported 200 bishops and archbishops and more
than 100000 priests, monks and nuns. The higher clergy lived lives of
luxury and wealth that not even the richest noblemen could match. In
the main city of Naples there were said to be 30000 beggars – one in ten
of the population. What had once been one of the most cultured and
civilised states of Europe in the middle ages had degenerated into one of
the poorest and most backward. Charles had to deal with problems far
greater than those faced by other Enlightened Despots.

The new King, a Spanish Bourbon, did not have the strong personal
links with enlightened thinkers that Frederick, Catherine or Leopold
enjoyed, but he was aware of their ideas. He was ably assisted in his
reforming programme by Bernardo Tanucci. Rising from obscure
origins and totally depending on the King for his power, Tanucci
started as Minister of Justice in charge of law reform, eventually
became Charles's Chief Minister, and finally became the effective ruler
of Naples when he was appointed Regent for Charles's baby son on

Charles's removal to Spain. Just how much the reforms owed to the work of this one minister became evident after his fall.

Charles's main interests at this time were in the arts, and his patronage of them is his chief claim to being considered an enlightened ruler at this time. Although unmusical himself, he was greatly interested in the opera, opening a new opera house in 1737 which rapidly became one of the most famous in Europe. Academies of art and design were established. The Roman cities of Pompeii and Herculaneum were discovered and Charles financed the archaeological work, although more, one suspects, to get his share of the treasures than from a love of history. He did, however, establish a Royal Academy at Herculaneum, the first to be devoted to archaeology. He was particularly interested in building, having a fine palace erected for him at Caserta, as well as a number of public buildings in Naples itself. Finally Charles also proved to be reformer in the field of higher education. The curriculum at Naples University was reformed. Theology made way for science, and his was the first university to start the teaching of economics.

Charles's patronage of the arts and education were complemented by Tanucci's more practical reforms. Tanucci was totally uninterested in the Enlightenment and had books by *philosophes* like Voltaire banned. He was interested in practical reforms, particularly those which strengthened royal power at the expense of the Church. However, in the 1730s he undertook a reform of the legal system, although it was modest by the standards of other rulers. It concentrated on improving prison conditions rather than reforming the penal code.

Tanucci made some attempt to improve conditions of the peasants. Serfdom was abolished, the peasants were allowed to sell their produce on the open market, and various unpaid personal services that the peasants had to undertake were abolished. However, the judges whose task it was to ensure that these reforms were obeyed were appointed and controlled by the nobles, and as a result of Tanucci's earlier failure to remove judicial authority from the nobles, the reforms were largely ignored. The peasants had to wait until the French invasion of 1798 for the power of the nobles over them to start to break.

Charles was a devout Catholic whose piety contrasts strongly with the cynicism of some of his fellow monarchs. Anti-clericalism was a major feature of the writings of the *philosophes*, and his lack of sympathy with their views makes his claim to be an Enlightened Despot difficult to sustain. Yet even Charles made reforms to the Church in Naples. A Concordat with the Pope in 1741 allowed him to start to tax the clergy, although their contribution remained small when compared to their wealth. The Concordat also allowed Charles to reduce the number of priests to 80000. At the same time the Church's judicial power and privileges were reduced. The Jesuits were expelled and Charles tried against enormous opposition to allow Jews into the state. When Charles left for Spain there had been a modest reduction in the power and wealth of the Church, but it remained one of the wealthiest and most privileged in Europe.

Charles was described at this time by the English ambassador as 'His own Minister . . . he has very high notions of his prerogative and thinks he is the most absolute monarch in Europe'. High notions and a genuine desire to do something for his subjects he may have had, but Charles's achievements after 29 years as ruler of Naples were modest. His reforms did not make major inroads into Neapolitan society, and Naples itself, a few fine palaces aside, remained a city of squalor and beggars in which thousands died of starvation in 1764.

Just how superficial his reforms were became clear after he left Naples to become King of Spain in 1759. Until 1771, while Tanucci acted as Regent, Charles's limited reforms were safe. After that year, however, the new King Ferdinand fell increasingly under the influence of his reactionary wife, Maria Carolina – Maria Theresa's daughter, but with none of her mother's good sense. By the time Napoleon's armies arrived to sweep away the *ancien régime* in Italy in the 1790s, virtually nothing remained of Charles's reforms.

The evils of Neopolitan society were so deep-rooted that only a ruthless and single-minded ruler could have eradicated them. Faced with far greater problems than Leopold had to deal with in Tuscany, it is not surprising that he failed. However, his time as ruler of Naples proved to be a useful apprenticeship for the more important work of ruling Spain.

4 Charles III: Spain 1759–88

Charles's phrase 'Everything for the people, nothing by the people' neatly sums up his attitude towards ruling Spain. On the whole his 30-year rule of Spain was more successful and had longer-lasting achievements than that of Naples. However, as in Naples, he was cautious about attacking the power of the Church and he showed little interest or sympathy for the view of the enlightened writers.

Charles was fortunate with his advisers. He had the ability to select a series of able administrators to help him throughout his reign. He never made the mistake of Frederick or Joseph of trying to run a large kingdom single-handed. Early in his reign he was shown the dangers of trying to move too fast for his conservative subjects. Free trade in grain coupled with a series of poor harvests led to a sharp increase in bread prices. These increases, combined with an attempt to abolish the traditional cloak and hat – which made it easy for a criminal to disguise himself – led to serious riots in Madrid in 1766. Charles's Chief Minister, the Marchese di Squillace, had already made himself unpopular because of Spain's poor showing in the Seven Years War. Now Charles was forced to sack Squillace and, for a time, had to flee from his capital. The riots alerted Charles to the dangers of an alliance between nobles and clergy on the one hand, anxious about protecting their privileges, and a superstitious and conservative peasantry on the other. It was the same problem that faced Leopold and Joseph. In later years Charles moved with greater care, but if the rioters thought they could persuade their King to abandon his reforms altogether, they were to be disappointed. Squillace was replaced as Chief Minister by the Count of Aranda. Within a year he had not only re-imposed the ban on the cloak, but blamed the riots on the Jesuits and had them expelled from Spain.

Despite the unfortunate statrt to his reign, Charles eventually gained the respect of his people by his genuine piety – essential in this land in which religious fanaticism was widespread – and by his exemplary private life. He was faithfully married to his wife and, even after she died, he remained faithful to her memory. For a King to provide such a good moral example to his people was unusual in the eighteenth century.

Charles's attitude to the Enlightenment remained equivocal. Although he praised the reading of literature and encouraged the long overdue reform of the curriculum at Spanish universities – until his reign some of them still taught that the earth was flat – most of the major works of the enlightened thinkers remained firmly on the Index and unavailable in Spain. The *Encyclopédie*, Montesquieu, Voltaire and Rousseau joined the works by Protestants condemned as dangerous and illegal books. Even books that were allowed, such as the writings of Beccaria, only appeared in Spanish translation many years later and seem to have aroused little interest. In Spain the books which excited much of Europe were either unavailable or unread. As a result, no intellectual class emerged to support the monarch in his reforming zeal as happened in some other states. Charles himself was not responsible for the books being banned since the Index was controlled by the Church, but neither did he attempt to have any of the books removed from the list. Judged by the criteria of awareness of and support for enlightened writers, Charles fails the test of Enlightened Despotism. When it came to practical measures, however, he achieved rather more.

With the Church Charles faced a formidable adversary. There were huge numbers of clergy – nearly 200000 of them – the highest percentage of the population of any country outside Portugal. Where Prussia had soldiers, Spain had priests. The Church was immensely wealthy and controlled all education. It controlled the Index, the Jesuits (until 1767), and the Inquisition – the most powerful of all such organisations. Even as late as the 1730s the *auto-da-fé* – where heretics or anyone who was critical of the Church was burnt at the stake in public – was a frequent occurrence. It sought out not only the small number of Protestants and Jews in Spain, but also anyone who questioned the authority, power or wealth of the Church. Both in its aims and methods it resembled the secret police force of some modern states, and was a formidable force resisting new ideas and reform.

Aranda was able to persuade Charles, on flimsy evidence, that the Jesuits had caused the 1766 riots. Their expulsion from Spain, following their earlier expulsions from Portugal and France, increased the pressure on the Pope to disband the unpopular organisation altogether. It was largely Charles's influence which persuaded the Pope to do this in 1773. The dissolution of the Jesuits was welcomed by the *philosophes*, who recognised the organisation as their most skillful and determined opponent. It was one of the few times that Charles did what the *philosophes* wanted, but in his case it was the Jesuit threat to royal authority, rather than their threat to free thought, which motivated him.

Charles was far more cautious about the Inquisition. He does not seem to have had strong views about it – 'The Spanish want it, and it does not bother me'. It lost its power to investigate the actions of royal officials and the number of *autos-da-fé* fell, but it was not abolished and remained popular with the people. Nor did it become a toothless dragon, as was shown in its successful prosecution of Don Pablo Olavide. Olavide was one of the few Spaniards who had close links with the enlightened writers. He was appointed by Charles to develop new villages. German immigrants were used for these new settlements, and the Church was deliberately left out of any say in the running of them. In fact the villages were not a success and Olivade proved to be a poor administrator. He had already resigned his post when he was arrested by the Inquisition. He was accused of reading banned books, writing to Voltaire, and possessing pornographic pictures. The first two charges were, of course, quite correct. The pictures consisted of some nude paintings by well-known artists. He was sentenced to eight years' detention in 1776, and was probably lucky to escape with his life. After four years he escaped to France and was acclaimed as the victim of religious intolerance by the *philosophes*. Clearly the Inquisition were hoping to send a warning to Charles about the advisers he chose. It is significant that Charles accepted the hint and made no attempt to save his ex-official. The trial was also a grim warning to anyone else who was tempted to read a book by Voltaire. If someone as senior as Olivade could be imprisoned so easily, there was no chance of an ordinary citizen escaping.

Major reforms were achieved in farming. A vigorous physiocratic approach was followed with some success. New areas were brought under cultivation, immigration was encouraged, and some royal land was distributed to peasants. Above all the government broke the power of the *Mesta*, the powerful group of sheep-farmers who for 300 years had enjoyed the right of pasture over extensive areas of Spain. Now at last that land could be used for more profitable growing of arable crops.

Similar progress was made in other areas of the economy. Roads and canals were built, the system of weights and measures was modernised, a postal system was established, internal customs duties reduced and the power of the guilds was broken. Charles made serious efforts to improve the status of industry and commerce in Spain. He tried to increase the respectability of trade by declaring that it was 'not degrading', and he made it legal for nobles to become merchants. Few nobles took advantage of the new law and their lack of interest revealed one of the most serious problems facing Charles in his attempts to reform Spain. Actually working for a living was considered dishonourable by many Spanish. Nobles considered it beneath their dignity, whilst the large numbers of beggars preferred to rely on charity from the Church. These were attitudes even Charles found impossible to overcome.

Despite all the difficulties, Charles did oversee some development in industry. In Valencia there were 4000 silk looms in the 1780s, whilst the cotton and woollen industries, freed from the restrictive practices of the guilds, quickly adopted the new technology being pioneered in Britain. As a result, by the 1780s only Britain had a larger textile industry. The development of the iron industry was stimulated by a law of 1775 banning imports. Charles also acted to encourage foreign trade, which had previously been controlled by a handful of privileged ports. By the end of his reign trade throughout the huge Spanish Empire was available to all Spanish ports, whilst at the same time most import duties were reduced. Foreign trade increased by about 500 per cent during Charles's reign. Although Spain still lagged significantly behind much of Europe in economic development, Charles could claim to have stimulated all sectors of the economy in line with the policies advocated by the *philosophes*.

Charles's attempts to improve the tax system were less successful. For many centuries the *Alcabala* (sales tax) had been the main source of government income, but its high rate made goods expensive. During his reign the tax rate was reduced by half. While this no doubt helped stimulate trade, Charles never attempted to remove the exemptions of the nobles and clergy from other taxes.

As King of Naples, Charles had already shown his interest in town development and the erection of fine public buildings. It is no surprise to find that in his years as King of Spain he did much to develop Madrid on the same lines. By the time he died he had helped turn his capital into an elegant city with public parks, a botanical garden and an observatory, and the schools, hospitals and almshouses which were now becoming the trademark of the Enlightened Despot.

Charles's foreign policy was moderately successful. He followed the traditional aim of conquering land and saw Great Britain as Spain's main rival for colonies and trade. At the start of his reign he made the mistake of allying with France in the Seven Years War. Spain lost Cuba and Florida, and with it much prestige. However, a reformed army and navy performed better in another war against Great Britain – the War of American Independence. At the Treaty of Versailles in 1783 Spain regained Florida and Minorca, which had been lost in 1713. Given the importance attached to success in foreign policy at this time, Charles could argue that Spain had recovered its strength after over 100 years of decline.

Charles had no links with the *philosophes* and had no wish to copy their ideas. Yet his own homespun philosophy came close to that which they were seeking in a monarch, as when he said 'I devote all my attention to improving the welfare of my subjects, since I wish to save my soul and go to heaven'. The *philosophes* would have agreed with his aims, if not with his reasons.

For the first for over 200 years Spain was fortunate enough to have a monarch who was willing to tackle her endemic problems – the power of the Church, the privileges of the nobility and the stifling of the economy. He had enjoyed only moderate success, and, like Maria Theresa, was prevented by his own piety from attacking the Church with more vigour. After his death, his unworthy successors allowed Spain to drift until, like so many other states, they were overwhelmed by the new forces coming from France.

5 Pombal: Portugal 1755–77

Sebastião José de Carvalho e Mello, better known as his later title of Marquis de Pombal, was the effective ruler of Portugal from 1755–77. He faced similar problems to Charles III, including economic decline, the power of the Church and extensive colonies which were more millstones than assets. However the differences between the two men are more striking. Pombal was a ruthless dictator who would not have been out of place in the twentieth century, while Charles was conciliatory. Pombal was not the King, and his power always depended on the total support he enjoyed from the monarch, the ineffective Joseph I (1750–77). Like other all-powerful ministers in the eighteenth century – Tanucci, Fleury, Potemkin, Kaunitz – he was in many ways a lonely person and could expect little sympathy if royal support was ever withdrawn. Pombal clearly felt there was no alternative to terror if he was to overcome opposition to his reforms. His apparent success shows just how much an Enlightened Despot could achieve if he were a true despot.

Pombal was born into a family of minor nobles. He married well and spent several years as a diplomat in Austria and England. He was particularly impressed by his stay in England. He admired the English system of government and its economic success. By contrast his own country had a huge but under-exploited colonial empire, poverty, ignorance and religious superstition. He was aware of enlightened ideas, but it is doubtful whether he was really a child of the Enlightenment. He preferred to read Molière from the previous century to the work of any recent writer. Joseph appointed him Minister of War and

Foreign Affairs at the start of his reign, but he did not become Chief Minister until the appalling Lisbon earthquake of 1755, which killed at least 10 000 people. Whilst the Church said that this was God's punishment for the sins of the people, Pombal's attitude was rather more realistic – 'Bury the dead and feed the living'. He supervised the rebuilding of Lisbon. Joseph was so impressed with Pombal's success that he virtually handed over power to him. Trusting him implicitly, Joseph rarely signed any decrees himself, leaving even this detail to Pombal. For the next 22 years Pombal was effectively the ruler of Portugal.

Pombal was bitterly hostile to the wealth and power of the Church which he saw was holding Portugal back. For some years his hand was restrained by the Queen Mother, but his chance came in 1758 with the Tavora conspiracy. A bungled attempt to murder Joseph may also have been designed to overthrow his unpopular Chief Minister. Pombal had Tavora, one of the most powerful nobles in Portugal, and many others arrested for the conspiracy. They were tortured and confessed. To this day it is not known if they were guilty. Certainly there must be suspicion that Pombal jumped at the chance to destroy once and for all the noble and clerical opposition to him. After a show trial Tavora and twelve others were brutally executed, some by being broken on the wheel. The medieval savagery of the tortures and executions contrasts strongly with his attempts to modernise and reform his state. The execution of this powerful noble certainly acted as a deterrent to others and there were no further attempts to overthrow him. Not satisfied with this, Pombal created the largest and most effective secret police force in Europe. Thousands were imprisoned, often without trial, for alleged opposition. Portugal lived in fear of its Chief Minister. Some 4000 political prisoners were released when Pombal finally fell from power in 1777. His regime was so brutal that the *philosophes* condemned it. He would have been quite at home in a twentieth-century totalitarian state.

The Tavora conspiracy also enabled Pombal to attack the Church. He seized on the suggestion that the Jesuits were involved in the conspiracy. He had also received complaints from settlers in South America about the way the Jesuits looked after the extensive lands they owned there. In fact, in areas like Paraguay the Jesuits had developed simple Christian communities where the Indians were treated with respect. In some places they had established communist communities where everyone shared the land and work. The colonists wanted the Indians as slaves and opposed the Jesuits who protected them. It is ironic that Pombal, who was later to abolish slavery altogether in the Portuguese Empire, at this stage chose to back the colonists in their quarrel. This suggests that he was looking for any excuse to destroy the Jesuits. Pombal had them expelled in 1759 and seized their lands and wealth. He was the first to attack the order, and his success encouraged Spain and France to follow suit. When the Pope conceded to pressure and abolished the Jesuits altogether in 1773, it was in many ways Pombal's greatest triumph. After the success of this first assault, Pombal renewed the attack on the Church. The Papal Nuncio was expelled, and no priests could be appointed without the approval of the government. Priests who dared to oppose him were imprisoned. Certainly he broke the power of the Church in Portugal, but there is one surprising omission in his attack. Although the Inquisition lost some of its power – it could no longer burn anyone without permission – it continued to exist virtually unaffected by the reforms. Since the Inquisition was no threat to Pombal and possessed no wealth worth seizing, this suggests that Pombal was more interested in power than faith.

Pombal followed a mercantalist economic policy and imposed it on a sometimes reluctant merchant class. Wine was turned into a state monopoly. To discourage grain imports, restrictions were placed on them whilst farmers were given inducements to grow grain instead of grapes. The state founded textile factories and at the same time banned textile imports. However, despite all his effort, Portuguese foreign trade remained firmly in foreign hands. In 1780 80 per cent of Lisbon's shipping was foreign owned – about the same figure as before Pombal came to power.

Perhaps Pombal's greatest achievement was his realisation of the need for future generations of trained people. He established a state education system far better than that of any other country in Europe other than Austria. Grammar schools were opened in all the main towns of Portugal, and teaching was to be in Portuguese instead of Latin. In 1772 he instituted a major reform of Portugal's main university at Coimbra, adding new departments of Mathematics and Science and having extensive new buildings added, including laboratories, a museum, an observatory and botanical gardens.

His other reforms also conform with the impression of a ruler following enlightened ideas. The tax system was modernised and government service was opened to all on the basis of merit, not birth. Jews were allowed to settle in Portugal and enjoyed full civil rights. A start was made on reforming the legal system. Slavery was abolished throughout the Portuguese Empire.

This appearance of enlightenment is misleading. Pombal had no interest in the *philosophes*. Having seized control of censorship from the Church, he used his powers to ban the works of Locke, Hobbes, Voltaire, Rousseau and Diderot. He was uninterested in any theory that questioned the right of a ruler to total obedience from his subjects. Even his justly admired education reforms were designed to create an educated and efficient middle class – they offered nothing for the peasants, for whom Pombal did little during his rule.

In 1777 Joseph died. The day after his death Pombal was curtly informed 'Your Excellency no longer has anything to do here' and was dismissed from all his posts. The new ruler was Joseph's daughter, Maria. She at once released the political prisoners, restricted the powers of the political police, abolished some of Pombal's trading companies and returned censorship powers to the Church. Pombal, now exiled to his estates, was bitter at the undoing of his work by this reactionary Queen. But actually he had little real reason to complain. She retained most of the former ministers and had actually dismantled relatively little of his work. She refused, for instance, to allow the Jesuits back and she could have gained easy popularity by executing him. However, after Pombal's death in 1782 the reaction speeded up. The nobility recovered much of its lost power. During the 1790s her son John went even further, restoring to the Church much of its lost wealth and power. By the time Napoleon's army marched into an undefended Portugal in 1807, virtually all of Pombal's achievements had been lost.

Pombal tried to turn a backward agricultural society into a modern industrialised state modelled on Great Britain, but Portugal had neither the resources nor the technology to succeed. He used torture and terror to impose his will at a time when other rulers were abolishing these methods. He was opposed to the ideals of the Enlightenment and made no attempt to assist the peasants. Seen in this light Pombal emerges as a dictator whose fall was greeted with delight by his people, and who could not possibly be termed an Enlightened Despot.

Yet in other respects Pombal, for all his faults and failures, does perhaps deserve the title. By weakening the Church and nobility, he helped to make it possible for a later generation of reformers to modernise Portugal in the nineteenth century. Alone amongst the rulers of Europe, he shared with the *philosophes* the vision of a society in which the middle class would assert its right to education, wealth and political office. He was the only ruler before 1789 to perceive the forces which would destroy the *ancien régime*.

6 Dr Struensee: Denmark 1770–72

Amongst the enlightened rulers of the eighteenth century, one of the most curious was Dr Struensee of Denmark. In a short rule of less than two years he achieved more than many others did in 20. Like Pombal, his power was based solely on his relations with the royal family, and like Pombal he fell in spectacular fashion when he lost that support.

Dr Struensee was not Danish. He was a Prussian doctor. It was increasingly unusual, but by no means unique for a foreigner to be appointed to a senior post in government. Other examples from this period include John Law (British) and Jacques Necker (Swiss) in France and Squillace (Italian) in Spain. Struensee was a keen follower of the Enlightenment. He had been particularly impressed by the works of Rousseau, although it is hard to discern any attempt to put Rousseau's theories into practice when he controlled Denmark. King

Christian VII (1766–1808), the third successive weak King of Denmark in the mid-eighteenth century, was mentally unstable and incapable of governing the country effectively. His wife, Queen Carolina Matilda (sister of George III of Great Britain) came to depend heavily on Dr Struensee, whose remedies seemed to have a beneficial effect on her husband. Just how the Prussian doctor kept the King's mental instability under control is not known; he may have used drugs. Whatever method it was, the Queen came to rely on him. By 1770 Dr Struensee was installed as the Queen's lover and the King's Chief Minister. The intensity of his reforming drive during the next 18 months suggests that perhaps he knew his time was bound to be limited.

First he had to break the opposition. He found himself in a similar situation to Leopold in Tuscany, ruling over a relatively prosperous country in which the nobility had long since lost its political power. Finding that the Privy Council was resisiting his laws, he simply abolished it and ruled by decree. He did not need to use torture, show trials, or secret police to enforce his rule as Pombal had. However, the relatively mild form of despotism he employed did not prevent him being unpopular or suffering the same sudden collapse of power as Pombal.

Once installed in office Struensee introduced an ambitious series of reforms. Press censorship was abolished – an act for which Voltaire singled him out for praise. He established a commission of inquiry into peasant grievances and then abolished serfdom. He overhauled the administration, making it both smaller and more efficient, and cut official salaries. On the other hand, he greatly increased court expenditure, presumably to retain the favour of the Queen. The contrast between giving lavish parties at Court and cutting the salaries of officials aroused great resentment. His abolition of serfdom was welcomed by the peasants; less popular was his attempt to fix the maximum wages that workers could earn. This attempt to impose an incomes policy on the state proved to be both unpopular and easily evaded.

In social reform Struensee was well ahead of his age. As a doctor he was particularly interested in health and he established an excellent system of hospitals. He was also unusually liberal in his views on sexual morality. He removed all punishments for unmarried mothers, illegitimate children and adultery. Brothels were freed from police supervision and Denmark's first clinic for venereal disease was established.

In his short period as dictator Struensee issued over 1000 decrees reforming all aspects of government. Torture was abolished and the whole legal system was reformed and updated, including the establishment of equality under the law. Nobles lost nearly all their powers over the peasants. Denmark was turned into a free trade state, promotion by merit in the government and army was established, and complete toleration for all religions was decreed.

Most of these reforms aroused great opposition. Some of the opponents were predictable – officials and nobles. However, Struensee angered wide sections of the population by his religious reforms, by the wages decree, by the fact that he was the Queen's lover and, above all, by being a foreigner. Struensee could speak no Danish. All his decrees were published in German, and there was a feeling that he was trying to 'Prussianise' Denmark. Nobles and the many officials sacked as part of his economy drive were able to play on the anti-German sentiments of the Danes. Struensee, presumably because he felt confident about the total support of the King and Queen, ignored the growing opposition.

His fall came suddenly in 1772. The Queen Mother persuaded the captain of the King's bodyguard to arrest Struensee. Struensee was brutally executed in front of an enthusiastic crowd – another object lesson, along with Pombal, of how easy it was to overthrow an apparently all-powerful minister. Only Queen Caroline mourned him. She was divorced and sent into exile.

With Struensee's fall some of his work could be undone. The Privy Council was restored and serfdom was re-imposed. However, much of his work survived, and serfdom was finally abolished in the 1780s. Although his rule was brief, it was more effective than Pombal's because his ideas came to a country that was already more advanced than Portugal. The Danish Church was already much poorer, smaller and less influential than Portugal's and its power could be easily broken. As early as the 1750s the Danish government had been actively working to lighten the burden on peasants, and the nobles had lost much of their power during the reign of Frederick IV (1699–1730). Denmark had already adopted modern farming methods and kings had followed an effective mercantilist economic policy. During the seventeenth and eighteenth centuries Danish scientists, including the astronomer Tycho Brahe, were amongst the most important in Europe. Copenhagen was the first city in Europe to introduce street lighting, and a system of state primary schools had been started in the 1730s. Denmark had already been moving towards a more tolerant and enlightened form of government long before Struensee rose to power, and this certainly made his reforming work easier.

There is a strong implication, therefore, that enlightened policies could succeed only in countries which were already socially and economically advanced. Most of Struensee's work survived, despite the fact that his overthrow was apparently welcomed by nearly everyone, and despite the vigorous efforts of the nobles and officials to regain their lost status. Yet Pombal, who ruled Portugal for far longer and with far greater ruthlessness, achieved less and saw many of his decrees cancelled within a few years. The difference between the two men does not tell us anything about the ability of the two ministers, but a great deal about the nature of the countries they ruled.

7 Conclusion

A number of other states were also ruled by kings who, it can be claimed, put enlightened ideas into practice. Gustavus III ruled Sweden for 20 years after seizing power from the *Riksdag* (Parliament) in a *coup d'état* in 1772. He was aware of the ideas of the Enlightenment, being particularly impressed by the works of Montesquieu and the Physiocrats. From the former he adopted the idea of a written constitution – he was in fact the first ruler in Europe to introduce one – and from the latter he adopted his economic policies of free trade, a stabilised currency and ending the powers of the guilds. He liked to call his system of government 'Legal Despotism', which was the phrase the *philosophes* used to describe their ideal form of government. In common with other rulers he introduced religious toleration, extending this to Jews in 1782, reformed the law and ended press censorship. He was particularly interested in the promotion of Swedish culture, building opera houses, theatres and palaces on a lavish scale.

At first Gustavus seems to have been popular and needed no secret police or censorship to stifle opposition. However, after 1788 there was mounting opposition to his growing absolutism, the rise in taxation to pay for his palaces, and his increasingly aggressive, expensive and unsuccessful foreign policy. After one war with Russia in 1788 in which no land was gained, Gustavus in 1791 called for a crusade against the French Revolution. A rumour that he proposed to abolish the *Riksdag* altogether was the final straw. In March 1792 he was assassinated by a group of nobles at one of the masked balls he loved to organise.

Gustavus had been both enlightened and despotic; but not at the same time. His earlier years, when he ruled as a constitutional monarch and introduced wide-ranging reforms contrast with his later years of absolutism and foreign adventures. Despite receiving praise from Voltaire, there is no real evidence that his policies, other than his economic reforms, were motivated by a concern for the welfare of his people. He certainly aimed to give Sweden an efficient state and to revive its old power, and was by no means uninterested in promoting his own image as a wise and benevolent ruler. In a speech to the Swedish Academy in 1786 he made it clear that he expected Sweden's writers and artists to glorify him in their works – an attitude similar to that of Frederick and Catherine with regard to Voltaire.

It is perhaps significant that the spectacular murder of Gustavus – the only assassination of a king outside Russia in the period covered by this book – was caused by his foreign policy failures. This is a reminder that even in a period when monarchs were supposed to be much more conscious of their responsibilities to their people, foreign affairs remained the main yardstick by which rulers were judged – as Frederick, Catherine and Joseph would also have testified.

Another monarch who has been put forward as a model Enlightened Despot was Charles Frederick, the Duke of Baden, one of the small states of the Holy Roman Empire. He had an exceptionally long reign (1738–1811), and can therefore claim to be both the first and last Enlightened Despot, starting his work before Frederick II, and outliving all the other rulers classed as such. He was the only one still ruling his state when Napoleon conquered Germany in 1805–6. He abolished serfdom and encouraged farming, trade and industry. His country enjoyed religious toleration and there was no press censorship. In a sweeping legal reform, Charles Frederick abolished both torture and the death penalty. He was interested in education, the arts and science, and tried to found a German cultural academy called 'The German Patriotic Institute'. As with other Enlightened Despots, there was a strong paternal tone to his rule. He even decreed that the state had to educate its people 'against their will how to manage their own affairs'.

Charles Frederick was the only ruler to put into practice the physiocratic dream of abolishing all existing taxes and replacing them with a single land tax. It was not a success. However, his ideas were sufficiently in tune with those of the conquering French armies in 1805 for Napoleon to accept him as an ally, and for him to become a member of the Confederation of the Rhine with considerably increased lands.

In attempting to sum up the different policies and achievements of a number of rulers, some common themes are apparent. Ministers who worked for tame kings – Pombal, Squillace, Tanucci and Struensee – had the least security. It was all too easy for their work to be dismantled when they lost the favour of their royal patron, or to be used as a scapegoat for the monarch's unpopularity. Most vulnerable were the foreigners – Struensee and Squillace – who could expect hostility from the people even at the best of times. Monarchs who undertook their own programme of reform could rely more on the traditional loyalties of the people to their sovereign, although, as Gustavus and Joseph found, there were limits to this loyalty.

In general the most successful of the minor despots were those who ruled small and comparatively advanced states such as Tuscany or Baden. They avoided the mistake of Joseph and Gustavus of trying to do all the work themselves, but used ministers such as Gianni in Tuscany. Such rulers escaped the temptation to dabble in wars, and needed circumstances to be favourable to them. Amongst the requirements were a Church which had already lost much of its power, wealth and influence, and a nobility that was either powerless, or which could be persuaded to work in co-operation with the monarch. It also helped if the country was already socially and economically developed, as were Tuscany, Baden and Denmark.

	Penal Reform	Church	Finance	Economy	Education and Arts	Government	Foreign Policy
Leopold II of Tuscany, 1765–90	Abolishes torture, secret trials; Equality under law	1780 – Inquisition abolished; Attacks on wealth, power, rituals	Simplified, related to income	Free Trade; New farming methods; Guilds abolished		1782 Charter	Pacifist
Charles IV of Naples, 1734–59	Prisons reformed (Tanucci)	1741 – Concordat; Jesuits expelled		Serfdom abolished – ineffective	Opera; Academies; Archaeology; Universities	Increased absolutism	
Charles III of Spain, 1759–88		1767 – Jesuits expelled; Inquisition loses some power	Alcabala halved	Physiocratic approach; Mesta broken; Guilds abolished; Industry, trade	Universities; Schools; Public buildings		7 Years War; War of American Independence
Pombal of Portugal, 1755–77	Slavery abolished	1759 – Jesuits expelled; Church's power and wealth attacked; Jews tolerated		Mercantilist industry	Schools, Universities	1758 – Tavora Conspiracy; Dictator; Secret Police	
Struensee of Denmark, 1770–72	Censorship abolished; Torture abolished; Equality under law	Religious toleration		Serfdom abolished; Wages fixed; Free trade	Hospitals	Dictator; Council abolished	
Gustav III of Sweden, 1772–92	Censorship abolished	Religious toleration		Free trade; Guilds abolished	Opera; Theatre	Constitution; Later dictator	1788 – War with Russia; 1791 – Crusade against France

Summary   The Minor Enlightened Despots

By contrast, Enlightened Despotism was less successful where the ruler had to use force to browbeat the nobles and Church into submission – as Gustavus, Pombal and Struensee found. Where the Church still enjoyed considerable wealth and support, rulers either trod with caution, as did Charles III in Spain, and achieved little, or attacked the Church fiercely, as did Pombal and Leopold, and risk the consequences. Either way a powerful Church remained a major constraint on the success of enlightened policies. A backward social and economic system, as existed in Naples and Portugal, meant that any reforms would be little more than skin-deep. A final factor working against success was failure in foreign policy, as Gustavus found. Charles III in Spain was the only minor despot to walk the tightrope of being actively involved in wars and emerging with no loss of prestige. Enlightened Despotism seems to have worked more effectively in small, unimportant states than in the Great Power states like Prussia and Russia. It could well be that it never was an appropriate way of running a large, complex state, and even in a small country the circumstances had to be right for it to be a practical approach for a ruler to adopt.

Making notes on 'The Minor Enlightened Despots'

You are extremely unlikely to be asked to write in depth about any ruler from this chapter in an examination essay. This means that your notes need to be neither as detailed nor as comprehensive on individual rulers as they were on Frederick, Catherine and Joseph. Instead, your aim should be to find (i) appraoches and (ii) problems which these rulers shared in common. In order to do this, it will help to adopt identical note structures for each of the five rulers (or seven if you include Gustavus III and Charles Frederick) covered in the chapter, using the headings below. You can then use these notes to pick out similarities and differences between the rulers. The conclusion to the chapter may also suggest ways in which one can draw common conclusions from the policies of apparently very different rulers.

1. The State of the Country (political, social, economic, and religious) When the Ruler came to Power
2. Awareness of Enlightened Ideas
3. Domestic Policy (in each case explain: aims, policies and achievements)
3.1. Peasants
3.2. Church
3.3. Law reform
3.4. Government
3.5. Nobles

3.6. Economy (trade, industry, duties)
3.7. Taxation
3.8. The arts, science and culture
3.9. Education
4.   Foreign Policy (again: aims, policies and achievements)
5.   Overall Assessment
5.1. Success or failure?
5.2. Was he an enlightened despot?

Not all these headings will be appropriate for every ruler.

Answering essay questions on 'The Minor Enlightened Despots'

Questions solely on the minor despots are unusual, and you are most unlikely ever to be asked simply to discuss one of them. It is probable that you will be asked to compare them with each other, as in:

   1.   'Does the record of reformers in smaller countries such as Portugal, Denmark or the two Sicilies entitle them to be called enlightened?'

Or the question might be even broader, asking you to discuss all the Englightened Despots, major and minor, as in:

   2.   'Which eighteenth-century ruler best merits the description "Enlightened Despot"?'
   3.   'Does Pombal represent the best example of eighteenth-century Enlightened Despotism?'

Question 2 is clearly the most general. No clues are offered by the examiner as to which rulers are to be covered. The first requirement for this (and the other) essays is that you must be able to offer a clear and concise definition of 'Enlightened Despotism'. Prepare your definition now, even though you might wish to modify it after you have read the last chapter. It should not be longer than three sentences. Having a clear definition will not only provide you with a ready-made introduction to one of these essays, but will be your essential yardstick by which to judge each of the rulers. You now have a choice of three approaches to the main part of question 2:

a) *Either* go through ruler by ruler, seeing which one best fits your definition. Your conclusion will identify (with reasons) which ruler is the best candidate for the title.

b) *Or* select your best candidate in advance, write about him or her in more detail, explaining how and why he or she fits your definition best, and then spend the second half of the essay briefly describing some of the other rulers explaining why you did *not* choose them.

c) *Or* go through the definition, with a paragraph on each topic (e.g. helping the peasants, law reforms), and see which ruler best fits that part of your definition. Your conclusion will sum up which ruler has come closest to achieving the ideals laid down in your original definition. Which topics would you include if you adopted this approach?

Each of these approaches has advantages and disadvantages.

The first has the advantage of dealing with one ruler at a time – the same way as your notes have generally been organised. It is easy to plan, but runs the risk of being dominated by narrative and 'not seeing the wood for the trees' – being so concerned with the ruler that the overall definition of Enlightened Despotism and a clear answer to the question only emerges right at the end, if at all.

The second approach has the advantage of keeping the question clearly in mind and devoting most space to the strongest candidate for the title. However, it requires the greatest planning since you are committing yourself to your answer before you start, rather than working out your answer as you go through the rulers.

The third approach is the most challenging and interesting. A thematic approach will keep your essay closest to the definition, although it can be quite difficult to handle a situation in which you have references to particular rulers scattered throughout the essay.

These issues would be highlighted if you prepared essay plans, according to the three approaches, for question 2 above. The examiner will give credit for a well-written answer using any of these methods, although the highest marks will probably go to a good answer using the third approach. Which approach do you find easiest to use? Why? Which ruler do you think comes closest to your definition of Enlightened Despotism? Compare your decision with those of the rest of your group. Did you all agree? If you did, you have done better than historians who have spent the last 200 years discussing this subject without reaching any consensus.

The two other questions will require a similar approach, despite the fact that the examiner has helpfully supplied some names of rulers. Any ruler so identified must be given due emphasis in the essay, but you must also offer comparisons with other rulers, or your answer will be incomplete. In question 3, for example, you will still need your definition of Enlightened Despotism to start with, followed by a discussion of Pombal's policies compared to the definition, and ending with a comparison with other rulers who might challenge his claim to be 'the best example'. An answer that deals exclusively with Pombal is likely to score poorly. So, in any essay such as this, you will need to make some sort of judgment as to how much of the essay should be devoted to the named individual(s), and how much to comparing him (them) with the other unnamed examples. In answering question 3, roughly what proportion of the essay would you devote to Pombal?

CHAPTER 7

Conclusion

1 Enlightened Despotism

The phrases 'Enlightened Despotism' and 'Enlightened Absolutism' were in use during the eighteenth century, but none of the rulers discussed in this book were given these titles during their lifetimes. The idea that there were kings called Enlightened Despots was an invention of nineteenth-century historians, and different historians have awarded the title to different rulers according to their own definitions. The title has, at various times, been given to rulers as contrasting in time, place and attitude as Louis XIV of France, Peter the Great of Russia, Napoleon, General de Gaulle and Mrs Thatcher. If the concept is to have any value, a more narrow definition is necessary than merely that of a strong ruler who claimed to be acting on behalf of his or her people.

The definition accepted by most historians is that there were a group of monarchs in the eighteenth century who were aware of and influenced by the theories being put forward by the writers known as the *philosophes*, and that these monarchs put some of these theories into practice. The policies adopted by such rulers included the standardisation and codification of laws; ending the use of torture and barbaric punishments; taking steps to protect the welfare of those unable to protect themselves; reducing the privileges and wealth of the established church and granting religious toleration; encouraging industry, trade and agriculture through the adoption of new techniques and by reducing restrictions and tariffs; patronising the arts and sciences; extending educational opportunities; helping the peasants; and ending some of the superstitions and mysteries attached to the institution of monarchy itself. Finally, in order to achieve this impressive reform programme, the Enlightened Despot would take steps to increase his or her own power at the expense of the nobles and the Estates. This power was used, not for self-aggrandisement or enjoyment as Louis XIV had done, but in order to benefit the state and its people.

The use of this definition rules out monarchs such as Peter the Great, who died before the *philosophes* started their work, and rulers after 1789 whose policies were influenced by factors other than the writings of Voltaire or Rousseau.

2 Philosophers and Kings

The first complication with this simple definition of Enlightened Despotism is that none of the *philosophes* actually advocated the range of policies listed above. As we have seen, the writers encompassed a wide range of different ideas and beliefs. Most of them, including two of the most famous, Voltaire and Diderot, came out with no new political philosophy at all. Both were sympathetic to absolute monarchy, but neither ever wrote a book of political philosophy advocating Enlightened Despotism as the ideal form of government. The writers who did discuss the ideal form of government – Rousseau and Montesquieu – both advocated quite different systems involving a monarchy shorn of power. It is therefore quite wrong to think of these writers as the philosophers of Enlightened Despotism in the same way as Bossuet, who had established a theoretical justification of Divine Right monarchy in the seventeenth century.

The *philosophes* were, in general, less interested in particular methods of government, than in the principles by which societies should be organised. Most of them wanted to see a society run according to rational scientific principles rather than religious dogma and rules. They felt that man was a rational being and that, through self-knowledge and the abandonment of superstition, it was possible for mankind to progress towards a happier and more prosperous existence. They contrasted their own age with the centuries before and decided that from the fall of the Roman Empire until their own times, Europe had descended into the Dark Ages of ignorance and superstition – an attitude towards the Middle Ages which we now know to be vastly over-simplified, but one which was flattering to the people of the eighteenth century, then entering the new world of reason, progress and knowledge. Although not fundamentally anti-Christian – they all claimed a belief in God – their beliefs led them into conflict with the churches, particularly the Roman Catholic Church. The *philosophes* rejected the Church's claim to hold a monopoly of both knowledge and morality. The Roman Catholic Church was aware of the threat and worked hard to have their books banned. In France, the home of the *philosophes*, they were unsuccessful. The Church's failure to get the *Encylopédie* banned was a significant defeat, and was soon followed by the expulsion of the Jesuits from France in 1764. In many ways the *philosophes* were more involved with their eventually successful campaign against the Church than in establishing an ideal form of government.

The *philosophes* have been criticised for their sycophancy towards monarchs. While denouncing abuses of power and advocating a greater concern for the rights and welfare of ordinary people in one hand, they excessively flattered some of the most ruthless monarchs on the other. Voltaire and Diderot were the worst offenders, but nearly all the writers at different times sought patronage in this manner. They put their considerable literary gifts at the disposal of these monarchs. The writers flattered for a purpose. In return they could hope both for protection from their own government, and the opportunity to have their ideas realised. The writers saw the monarchs as the only group of people capable of putting reforms into practice. A little insincere flattery was a small price to pay to see their ideas become reality. The writers felt that they were using the monarchs for their own purposes, and Voltaire openly admitted that this was what he was doing.

The monarchs in turn were not stupid. They enjoyed the flattery and the prestige of patronising such famous writers. They could use the writers to act as propagandists for them in Europe, and this is particularly noticeable in the way Catherine II used Voltaire to create an image of a civilised, sophisticated Russian monarchy, so unlike the old idea that Russia was a land of barbarism and backwardness presented by Peter the Great. In a moment of candour Catherine admitted 'Do you know that it was Voltaire who made me the fashion?'. Meanwhile the monarchs could pick and choose those aspects of the writers' policies which suited them, while rejecting those which were inconvenient or which might reduce their power.

The evidence suggests that the monarchs got the better of the deal. Writers did not hesitate to justify or ignore the most unsavoury aspects of their patrons' conduct. We find the writers justifying the casual rape of Poland in 1772 on the grounds that the three robber monarchs were bringing the blessings of religious toleration to the ignorant peasants of Poland. Voltaire dismissed Catherine II's murder of her husband, Peter III, as 'family matters' which were none of his business. The *philosophes* held much the same position as court jesters in the Middle Ages – their job was to amuse and entertain their royal patrons, and they might even criticise from time to time so long as this did not get out of hand.

All this suggests a one-sided relationship between cynical monarchs and naive writers. This is rather too simple. The fact that monarchs felt it necessary and desirable to patronise critical writers, or that monarchs were aware that they would make useful propagandists, is itself an indication of the writers' increasing influence in educated circles. Catherine and Frederick did not just patronise writers so that they could use them. They had both demonstrated an interest in their writings and ideas long before they came to power, so it is reasonable to assume that there was also a genuine interest in the ideas and a willingness to see some of them introduced.

The relationship between monarchs and writers was based on some common beliefs, but there were also more cynical motives on both sides, *philosophes* and monarchs needed and used each other. It was a relationship that suited them both.

3 Royal Policies

During the eighteenth century monarchs had been able to justify their existence and powers partly on the practical grounds that the alternative, rule by nobles, was worse, and partly by theory of the divine right of kings. The latter justification was increasingly discredited during the eighteenth century, while the rise of Holland and England suggested that there were successful alternatives to absolute monarchy. It is sometimes argued that monarchs turned to Enlightened Despotism as a way of justifying their own existence. In fact there is no evidence that monarchs felt they had to do this, or that they felt threatened. On the contrary, it was an age of self-confident monarchy, where kings did not hesitate to add to their power and to antagonise powerful groups. Even a king as lazy and unambitious as Louis XV of France could confidently crush the opposition of his *parlements* in 1770 to a reform of the judicial system. Joseph II is a further example of a monarch who felt his personal authority alone was sufficient to ensure obedience from all his subjects. Even George III of England tried to increase his power – or so his actions were perceived both by his American colonists in their Declaration of Independence, and by the English House of Commons when they passed Dunning's motion in 1780 denouncing the growth of royal power. The argument that monarchs introduced enlightened policies in order to justify their own existence seems unconvincing. Why then did they do so?

4 Enlightened Despotism in Practice

That some eighteenth-century monarchs undertook wide-ranging prog- rammes of reform in line with the suggestions of the *philosophes* is undeniable. It does not follow, however, that it was these suggestions that led monarchs to undertake reforms. There are several examples of monarchs who totally rejected the ideas of the Enlightenment and had the offending books banned, while at the same time undertaking extensive reforms of the sort encouraged by the same writers. Maria Theresa, for example, made important reforms to the administrative, judicial and educational systems of her empire. She also made tentative reforms in the field of finance, economics, religion, education and serfdom. The scope and extent of her reforms might qualify her as one of the most successful of the Enlightened Despots – except that she was completely hostile to the Enlightenment. In her case she was obliged to reform in order to modernise her state in the face of the threat from Frederick the Great, a monarch who is always accorded the title of Enlightened Despot, but one who actually did rather less to modernise his state than Maria Theresa. Frederick William I of Prussia is another example from the eighteenth century of a monarch who successfully modernised his state while being hostile to the Enlightenment. In his case he paid particular attention to centralising the government and overhauling the tax system, with more token efforts in the fields of education and serfdom. These examples indicate that extensive reforms were possible in the eighteenth century without any debt to the Enlightenment. The motive was solely the strengthening of the state.

Another group of rulers, including Pombal in Portugal, Charles III in Spain and Tanucci in Naples, undertook ambitious programmes of reforms while at the same time banning the works of the *philosophes* and suppressing any manifestations of opposition to the existing political system. In these cases they did not only use the argument of strengthening the state to justify their reforms, but also their wish to look after their subjects and end abuses of power by nobles and clergy. In each case the ruler was aware of the ideas of the Enlightenment and put both their aims and policies into practice, while suppressing the books themselves.

Finally there existed a number of monarchs, notably Frederick II, Catherine II, Joseph II and Leopold, who not only introduced enlightened reforms, but also freely acknowledged their debt to the *philosophes* and allowed their writing to be available in their states. Even in these cases this evidence does not, in itself, prove that their reforms were motivated by enlightened ideas. We have seen that there was certainly an element of the monarchs using the *philosophes* for their own purposes, and this has led some historians to argue that their policies in fact owed nothing to the writers, but would have taken place anyway.

According to this view monarchs had, for several centuries, been accumulating power in the form of bureaucracies and armies at the expense of the nobility. The reforms of the 'Enlightened Despots' often followed logically from their earlier centralising policies, and owed far more to these than to any books. It was the state which mainly benefited when noble and Church privileges were reduced and their income taxed; the extra income was almost invariably used to fight wars rather than to care for the people. Even such apparently paternal acts of welfare as providing schools benefited the state. Schools ultimately increased the nation's wealth by producing a skilled workforce, and the young would, moreover, be indoctrinated in loyalty to their monarch rather than to their religious faith, as in former times. It was the state that benefited from increased prosperity when trade and industry were freed from the shackles of the guilds or when new roads and canals were built. Enforcing religious toleration reduced the danger of internal conflicts and encouraged immigration.

It was not necessary to read Voltaire to see the advantages of these policies; reading Machiavelli would do just as well. Using the language of the Enlightenment gave credibility to policies which were designed to increase the monarchs' own power. These rulers were neither better nor worse than their predecessors in their ambitions; they were, however, more sophisticated in the way they justified their actions.

This argument, although not without some justification, is based on a misunderstanding of the nature of the Enlightenment. It is incorrect to claim that a policy which strengthened the state could not be enlightened. Neither the monarchs, nor most of the writers saw any contradiction between state power and enlightened reform; on the contrary, the one could only be achieved by the other. Enlightened thinkers were certainly in favour of ordinary people enjoying the maximum possible freedom, including the right to worship, work and write without restriction. At the same time most *philosophes*, including Voltaire and Rousseau, favoured an increase in state power as an essential part of their programme. The two would complement each other at the expense of noble selfishness and clerical superstition.

If it is misleading to think that increased state power negated the ideals of the Enlightenment, it is also too simple to see the monarchs as cynical manipulators, merely using the writers as propagandists while they continued to practise policies they would have followed anyway. There are a number of specific instances where reform did follow the publication of a book. The best example is Beccaria's book on punishments, which led directly to penal reform in Austria, Prussia, and Russia – in each case the debt to Beccaria being freely admitted. The Physiocrats had an influence on economic policy in Austria, France, Baden and elsewhere towards the end of the period. The *philosophes*' successful challenging of the Roman Catholic Church in France helped lead to various governments expelling the Jesuits and in other ways asserting their authority over a previously powerful institution. The impetus of humanitarian reform can also be seen in the first moves towards the abolition of the slave trade, a rare victory in the history of Europe of moral principle over convenience and profit. These were real achievements for the *philosophes*, although much less than they had hoped for. Both Voltaire and Rousseau expressed regrets towards the end of their lives that they had not achieved more. Although the instances where there is a clear link between the books and practical reform may seem as modest today as they did to Voltaire and Rousseau, the Enlightenment's influence was more widespread. Frederick, Catherine and Joseph were all deeply influenced by the enlightened books they read when they were young. Much of their life's work and their attitude towards their subjects was in turn influenced by this education. The *philosophes* were actually changing attitudes amongst monarchs far more than they themselves realised.

5 Enlightened Foreign Policy

For most rulers a successful foreign policy remained a major preoccupation of their reign. The need to defend the state from enemies and to expand, where possible, its borders and power, were both a justification for the monarch's existence, and the main yardstick by which they were judged by their own people and by foreigners. The few rulers, like Frederick William of Prussia or Leopold of Tuscany, who carefully avoided wars, were regarded as eccentric. Wars were normal and expected, and these were very few years during the eighteenth century when there was not a war taking place somewhere in Europe.

It may appear surprising, therefore, that the *philosophes* paid relatively little attention in their books to war and foreign policy. It is true that when they did, the practice of war was generally criticised. Only two lesser-known writers, Saint-Pierre in 1713 and Price in 1776, actually suggested preventing wars completely by setting up an international peace-keeping force. They, alongside the German writer Kant, opposed war on principle. Other writers did not object to wars on principle, but did deplore some of its effects. The Physiocrats objected to the way war disrupted the economy, Montesquieu denounced the arms race, and Voltaire in *Candide* poured scorn on the harshness of military discipline and the way in which wars perverted men's sense of honour. Nearly all the writers condemned wars undertaken purely for personal glory or for greed. They preferred monarchs to concentrate on helping their people rather than on the irrational pursuit of honour.

There is a stark contrast between the writers' reservations about wars and the reality of the eighteenth century. The second half of the century was dominated by wars started by monarchs who called themselves enlightened. The *philosophes*, far from condemning these campaigns, were usually to be found actively supporting them. How did this happen?

Eighteenth-century wars were fought for a variety of motives. Religious disputes, except perhaps in the case of Russia and the Ottoman Empire, were no longer a major cause of war. Only an old-fashioned monarch like Louis XV would fight a war for family or dynastic reasons – in 1733 he went to war with Austria in order to help his father-in-law become King of Poland. Increasingly wars were caused by personal ambition, territorial conquest, or for trade and colonies. Personal ambition had always been a cause of war, but eighteenth-century monarchs were much more open about this. Frederick II in particular was not ashamed to admit that he attacked Austria in 1740 because of 'ambition and the desire to make a name for myself'. Catherine II also started wars for personal reasons, in her case because a successful foreign policy would bolster her own position at home. Similarly, Joseph II's wars against Bavaria and Turkey were at least partly motivated by the need to be seen as being as successful a general as Frederick II.

The wish for territorial conquest was another major reason for going to war. From Frederick II's attack on Silesia down to the Third Partition of Poland in 1795, the Great Powers sought to take land from weaker states. Such aggression was justified by *raison d'état*: anything that strengthened the state was right, and weak countries deserved to lose their land because they had allowed themselves to decline. Joseph justified Austria's participation in the First Partition of Poland (1772) on the grounds that the conquest of Galicia would be compensation for the loss of Silesia. Maria Theresa, being an old-fashioned ruler with some moral principles objected on the grounds that Poland had done Austria no harm. Joseph, representing the new rational approach to foreign policy, was supported by Kaunitz and eventually overcame his mother's objections.

The last factor, trade and colonies, became increasingly important as a cause of wars, particularly those involving Great Britain. However, it is important to note that the Enlightened Despots never fought wars purely for commercial reasons. Silesia was attacked by Frederick primarily because of its proximity, rather than because of its useful mines. Indeed, with the exception of Silesia, much of the land conquered in wars at this time was of very little economic value to the conqueror.

Despite all the evidence that wars were being fought without the just causes that the *philosophes* argued were necessary, and despite the open cynicism of rulers like Frederick II with his remark 'One takes what one can. One is only wrong when one loses', the writers had no difficulty in justifying the most blatantly aggressive acts of their patrons. Thus we find Voltaire justifying Russian intervention in the First Partition of Poland on the grounds that it would bring the blessings of religious toleration to the Poles. In a similar vein his only regret when Catherine attacked Turkey in 1768 was that no other European state was helping her. He defended Frederick's attack on Silesia on the grounds that Prussian administration would be fairer and more efficient than Austrian. In private Voltaire and other *philosophes* were uneasy about these repeated acts of aggression, but at no time did they attempt to restrain or criticise their royal patrons. The writers do not emerge with much credit. Their attitude to their patrons' foreign policy was uncritical and syncophatic.

Does this mean that the Enlightenment had no influence at all on the foreign policy of monarchs in this period? Indirectly it did change attitudes towards war. No Enlightened Despot fought wars for such irrational reasons as dynastic ambition or religious crusade. They relied icreasingly on diplomacy as a preparation for war and, in at least one instance (The First Partition of Poland) as a means of avoiding a war. While wars remained frequent, they tended to become less destructive. Armies were now better disciplined and as a result were more likely to live off their own baggage train than loot the villages through which they passed. None of these features were a result of monarchs wishing to look after their subjects, but they were a result of a rational analysis of how the state could most efficiently expand.

Eighteenth-century Enlightened Despots fought as many wars as rulers in previous centuries. That they fought these wars in order to benefit the state and with as much efficiency as possible might be argued as some sort of progress. That they were more honest about their motives than rulers either before or since might be considered commendable. In general, however, the Enlightenment's vision of only strictly necessary wars seems to have had no discernible influence on the policies of the monarchs.

6 The Impact on the French Revolution

Almost as soon as the French Revolution began in 1789, much of the blame for its outbreak was put on the *philosophes*. Edmund Burke wrote the first analysis of the causes of the Revolution, *Reflections on the Revolution in France* in 1790, and pinned much of the blame on the subversive influence of the writers, who had undermined respect for religion and monarchy through their unceasing attacks on the *ancien régime*. The theory was further developed by the Abbé Barruel who in 1797 argued in his *L'histoire de Jacobinisme* that the Revolution had been caused by a conspiracy between the *philosophes* and freemasons. Although the conspiracy theory has not stood the test of time, the idea that the writers helped cause the Revolution has been repeated by many other historians, including Taine who wrote that 'Millions of savages were launched into action by a few thousand scribblers' (*L'Ancien Régime*, 1875).

In reality the links are not convincing. It is true, as we have seen, that the resistance to oppression was given credibility by the writings of the *philosophes*, and that the *parlementaires* had borrowed freely from the works of Montesquieu when they resisted Louis XV's attempt to destroy their power in 1770. However, as we have also seen, none of the writers, apart from Rousseau, were hostile to monarchy as such and none advocated democracy or revolution; Voltaire, who became a hero to the Revolution, and who was reburied as such in the Pantheon, was strongly opposed to both and therefore in no sense a supporter of the Revolution. Some of the writers were hostile to Louis XIV and Louis XV, but none wrote books critical of Louis XVI. The causes of the French Revolution were many and varied, but today few historians regard the influence of the *philosophes* as significant.

Although the writers were not responsible for starting the revolution, they did have some limited influence on its course. The 1791 Constitution owed a lot to the ideas of Montesquieu, as did the 1793 Constitution to Rousseau. However, the first only lasted for one year and the second was speedily replaced by the Reign of Terror, so neither can be said to have had a lasting impact on the course of the Revolution. Robespierre was influenced by Rousseau, and in his short-lived Republic of Virtue (1794) he did claim to represent the General Will. He was overthrown after only a few months, and the attempt has never been repeated. The French revolutionaries adopted popular sovereignty because with the collapse of royal authority in 1789, the only way government could be maintained was by transferring authority to 'The Nation' as represented by the National Assembly. Such a notion had never been advocated by any of the writers, but was a practical solution to the political crisis of 1789.

The Revolutionary governments did introduce a number of social reforms in line with enlightened ideas. These included the introduction of a state education system, the abolition of slavery, the ending of financial and other privileges for the Church and nobility, and the establishment of equality under the law. In general, however, the Revolution owed little to the *philosophes*, and it is likely they would have been appalled at its violence, the breakdown in social order, and its intolerance. Like the monarchs, revolutionary leaders proved to be adept at picking and choosing appropriate sections from the works of the *philosophes* to justify their actions.

A more important result of the Revolution was to discourage further experiments in enlightened reform in the rest of Europe. Both Catherine II and Joseph II were obliged to backtrack on their reforms in the face of the Revolution. The Austrian Emperor, Leopold, was the last monarch to believe that it was possible for Revolutionary France to co-exist with old Europe. By 1793 most of the major European states, including a number which had introduced reforms in recent years, had decided the Revolution threatened their existence and that it must be crushed. The result was a crusade on behalf of the *ancien régime* against the French Revolution, and an end to Enlightened Despotism. Catherine II was one of many monarchs who now banned the French books she had previously patronised. She shared with the Abbé Barruel the idea that the works of men such as Voltaire caused trouble and encouraged the masses to revolt. Voltaire's strange fate was to end up as the hero of the French Revolutionaries, whom he would have despised, and banned by the absolute monarchs he admired.

7 Historians and Enlightened Despotism

During the nineteenth century few historians doubted the existence of Enlightened Despotism. In the 1890s Lord Acton wrote *Lectures on Modern History* which included, in an essay on Frederick II, an influential interpretation.

1 The years that followed the Seven Years War were a time of peace for a great part of the continent, in the course of which a memorable change took place. It was the age of what may be called the Repentance of Monarchy. That which had been selfish,
5 oppressive and cruel became impersonal, philanthropic and beneficient. The strong current of eighteenth century opinion left the state omnipotent, but obliged it to take account of public rather than dynastic interests. It was employed, more or less intelligently, for the good of the people. Humanity contended for the
10 mastery with ambition. It was still despotism, but enlightened despotism. It was influenced by great writers – Locke, Montesquieu, Turgot, Beccaria, Adam Smith. There was a serious tendency to increase popular education, relieve poverty, build

hospitals, to promote wealth, emancipate the serf, abolish torture
15 and to encourage academies and the like. Attempts were made to
reform prisons. People began to doubt the morality of the slave
trade. Laws were codified. The movement was almost universal,
from Spain to Denmark and Prussia.

This view – that Enlightened Despotism had a real existence, was based
on the monarchs being 'repentant', and led to real progress in Europe –
remained until the 1920s when an International Historical Congress
initiated a more critical approach to the concept. Fritz Hartung's
Historical Association pamphlet (*Enlightened Despotism*, 1957) helped
give it its current narrow definition, limiting it to the eighteenth
century and to those monarchs aware of the writings of the *philosophes*.
Both Acton and Hartung singled out Frederick II for particular praise,
the former commenting that 'In the age of Enlightened Despotism, the
most enlightened despot was Frederick II'.

However, more recently historians have tended to be critical of the
whole concept. Greater stress is now placed on the ways that monarchs
used the *philosophes* for their own purposes, the extent to which their
policies owed less to the books than to the traditions of their own states,
and to their wish to increase their own power. Some have questioned
whether Enlightened Despotism existed at all. M. S. Anderson in the
first edition of *Europe in the Eighteenth Century* (1961) argued that it was
impossible to find any valid examples where enlightened ideas had
actually influenced the policies of the rulers, although in the second
edition he modified this line. In a similar vein, George Rudé, in a book
with the same title, argued that 'Enlightened Despotism, when it was
Enlightened, was almost universally a failure' and that 'Aristocracy and
privilege, so often the proclaimed target of Enlightened Despotism,
emerged from the whole experience strengthened rather than
weakened'.

Few historians today would be as dogmatic as Acton in asserting that
monarchs on the defensive changed their policies to something quite
new in the 1760s, but the claim that monarchs were totally unin-
fluenced by the Enlightenment is equally difficult to sustain. At the
moment Enlightened Despotism retains its place as a valid historical
concept.

8 Success or Failure?

The achievements of the Enlightened Despots varied from state to state
but were, in general, far more limited than the ambitious reform
programme envisaged by many of the writers. There were a number of
reasons for this. Many of the *philosophes* underrated the practical
problems of introducing widespread reform and assumed a general
willingness by people to accept change. This proved to be optimistic.

They underestimated the remaining strength of religious faith and the continuing influence exercised by the nobility. In addition, many of the monarchs themselves showed a greater interest in foreign conquest and strengthening the state than in humanitarian reform. Finally, even where radical reform was introduced, its success remained dependent on the ruler himself. A change often resulted in an immediate and popular dismantling of the recent reforms.

No ruler could claim to have enjoyed complete success in introducing reform, and many either attempted very little or were unsuccessful in more ambitious programmes. The best example of the failure of Enlightened Despotism remains Joseph II, who suffered the particular humiliation of being the only monarch forced to abandon his reforms in his own lifetime. Historians still argue as to why Joseph's attempts failed, but whatever the reasons his failure shows the difficulty in imposing reforms from above on a hostile population. As well as being a personal failure for Joseph, his reign also suggests the failure of the *philosophes* to anticipate the extent of opposition to reforms.

In contrast to Joseph, the much more limited reforms of Frederick II and Catherine II lasted much longer. Both Frederick and Catherine took particular care to cultivate the friendship of the writers, perhaps because this would help disguise their failure to introduce real reforms into their states. However, it was precisely their caution that enabled more of their work to survive. Both took care not to antagonise the nobles and to limit their reforms to less controversial areas than freeing the serfs or introducing universal state education. Frederick's reforms lasted until the collapse of Prussia in 1806. When the state was recreated after the Battle of Jena, elements of Frederick's Prussia were retained. Even more lasting were Catherine II's reforms. The attempt of her son, Paul, to undo her work after she died ended with his own murder in 1801. Later Russian rulers made no attempt to change her system of government and society until the abolition of serfdom in 1861. In many ways even the Russia of 1917, and in particular its system of government, was essentially unchanged from that of Catherine II. She was not perhaps the best example of Enlightened Despotism, but she was certainly the most successful.

Much of the success or failure of enlightened reform depended on the reaction of different groups of people to them. Noble opposition to reforms which threatened their wealth and status was to be expected. What was surprising was the skill and energy with which they resisted reform. Pombal and Joseph II aroused particular hostility from their nobles. The nobles showed they were able to use sophisticated methods to resist reform, both by combining forces with the peasants, and by using the arguments of the *philosophes* themselves to justify resistance to oppression. We find the nobles of Hungary, the Austrian Netherlands, Poland and France quoting Montesquieu and Rousseau to explain their opposition to proposals that would strengthen the authority of the state.

In the eighteenth century, rulers could not manage their states without the co-operation and help of the nobility. Their own bureaucracy was still too small and inexperienced to substitute for the nobles. Monarchs who openly challenged the nobles failed. Monarchs who avoided challenging the nobles found they could achieve many of their other reforms. The continuing strength of the nobility is one of the more surprising features of late eighteenth-century Europe.

Peasant opposition was another major factor which the writers had ignored. They had assumed that ordinary people were pliable and would welcome reforms designed to benefit them. Many rulers, and Joseph II in particular, shared this misconception. Yet in many states peasants resisted reform as vigorously as did the nobles. This peasant opposition was neither short-sighted nor insincere. Peasants were deeply suspicious of the state with good reason. To them the state was represented by the tax collector and the recruiting sergeant. When the state proposed changing their farming methods, forcing their children into schools and altering their church services, there was opposition which the nobles and Church found easy to exploit. At this time there was no concept of the state being there to protect its citizens, and none of the rulers felt it necessary to explain to the peasants their reasons for change. All that peasants wanted from the state was to be left alone. The opposition of the peasants to reform was one of the main reasons for the failure of Enlightened Despotism in Austria, Spain and Naples. Monarchs like Catherine II who allowed the condition of the peasants to deteriorate could also expect peasant hostility. The most successful approach was that of Frederick II, who, through a cautious paternalism, was able to avoid popular uprisings throughout his reign.

Church opposition was an important factor in Spain, Austria, Naples, Portugal and Tuscany. The writers won important victories over the French Catholic Church, but this was a Church that had already been subordinated to state power by previous monarchs. Protestant and Orthodox Churches posed no threat to the monarchs as they had been under complete state control for many years. The Protestant Church, moreover, was not opposed to many of the ideas put forward in the Enlightenment. However, in the more backward areas of Europe the Roman Catholic Church still enjoyed considerable power and support, and was able to put up strong opposition to royal reforms. When united with nobles and peasants, the combination was a formidable obstacle to reform.

Enlightened Despotism, when genuinely enlightened, aroused far greater opposition than the writers or rulers had anticipated, and in every case the opposition was ultimately successful in resisting reform. Where monarchs restricted themselves to administrative reform, or in states where conditions were more favourable to reform, a measure of success was possible. Favourable conditions included a nobility already weakened, a Church, preferably Protestant, under state control, a large middle class sympathetic to reform, and a peasantry which had long since ceased to be serf-bound. Such conditions only existed in a handful of western European states.

Of the best-known Enlightened Despots, Joseph II was both the most genuinely enlightened and the least successful. Frederick II showed the greatest skill in dealing with the peasants, but in other respects does not seem to deserve the praise heaped on him by earlier generations of historians. Catherine II was unsuccessful with the peasants and was the most cynical exploiter of the propaganda value of the *philosophes*, yet her reforms were the longest lasting. None could claim to have reached the position of the successful Philosopher-Prince of which Voltaire and the other writers dreamt.

The Enlightenment was an important intellectual movement of the eighteenth century, with a limited influence on the policies of many rulers. Enlightened Despotism had a real existence, although it achieved less than either the writers or the genuinely enlightened rulers had hoped for. None of the rulers was able to solve the contradition inherent in Enlightened Despotism: the paradox of a ruler seeking to help his people whilst at the same time destroying their old way of life and ignoring their wishes.

The French Revolution swept away old Europe and suggested that Enlightened Despotism was part of an archaic system of government, inevitably overtaken by progress. Yet the French Revolution did not automatically lead to progress and freedom, and the last century has seen many nations turn to new types of despotism, always claiming to act on behalf of and with the consent of the people, but subject neither to the religious restrains of seventeenth-century monarchs nor the moral restraints of those of the eighteenth century. Compared to what they had experienced before 1740 and what happened after 1789, the people of Europe in the mid-eighteenth century were generally fortunate to have been ruled by those monarchs who historians label the Enlightened Despots.

Making notes on 'Conclusion'

Your notes should enable you to take a broad overview of the impact of the Enlightenment, and the extent to which Enlightened Despotism existed in eighteenth-century Europe.

Your first step, if you have not already done so, should be to write a definition of Enlightened Despotism in about three sentences. This should be brief enough to remember for use in essays, and will be the yardstick by which you judge the rulers.

Next, draw up a table for each of the three major rulers covered in chapters 3, 4 and 5. Divide your page into four quarters. In the top left-hand box briefly summarise the arguments for saying that a particular ruler was an Enlightened Despot, and on the top right the arguments against. The bottom left-hand box should summarise his or her successes in domestic policy, and the bottom right-hand his or her failures. This exercise should provide you with a useful basis for the types of assessment required in comparative essays.

Answering essay question on Enlightened Despotism in general

In this section we will look at two types of essay: those asking for a comparison between two or more of the major 'Enlightened Despots', and those which ask very general questions about the whole theory and practice.
    Examples of the first type are:

1. 'In what ways was Emperor Joseph II less successful than Frederick II?'
2. 'Compare Catherine II and Joseph II as "Enlightened Despots".'
3. '"Despite their good intentions, neither Catherine nor Joseph achieved very much for the welfare of their people." Discuss.'

The wording of these questions suggests that the examiners are aware that it is unreasonable to expect you to write comprehensive accounts of the reigns of two rulers in a single essay. Questions 1 and 3 limit the amount of ground to be covered by identifying particular aspects of the reigns to be considered. Which aspects are these? By now, you should be able to prepare a series of paragraph headings to cover the appropriate topics. You should also be aware that it would probably be a mistake to deal first with one ruler and then with the other, and that you should seriously consider tackling the question by topic or theme. Which topics would you select for each essay?
    Question 2 is more wide-ranging, but it is also more straightforward. In fact, it is identical in approach to some of the questions discussed on page 142. Use your three-sentence definition of Enlightened Despotism to plan a series of paragraphs dealing with different aspects of your definition, and see how well each ruler fits into it.
    The second type of question covers the general theory and practice of Enlightened Despotism, such as:

4. '"Power, not welfare, was the guiding principle of Enlightened Despotism." Discuss with reference to one or more eighteenth-century rulers.'
5. 'With what justification can the eighteenth century be described as an "Age of Reason"?'
6. 'What central ideas do you associate with the French *philosophes*

and for whom was their message intended?'
7. 'How valid is the claim that European writers of the eighteenth century were invariably against the established order?'

Faced with a general question such as one of these, your first instinct might well be to choose another question on the examination paper. The examiners often comment sadly on the unpopularity of essays like these. However, although they are certainly less accessible than most of the questions that concentrate on just one ruler, you should now be in a position to tackle them, by working through the following steps:

a) Start by carefully studying the wording of the question and decide exactly what is being asked of you. It sometimes helps to spend a few minutes 're-wording' the question, so as to create a series of more manageable questions which will assist you in identifying which aspects of the topic are actually being asked about.

You may remember that most essay questions are of one of three types. Awareness of these types should help you to identify what is required in your answers. The three types are:

  i) The 'challenging statement', usually, but not always, in the form of a quotation. With such questions, you should carefully study the statement so as to identify both the topic and the particular viewpoint that the examiner wants you to discuss.
  ii) 'How far/to what extent' questions. These require a similar approach as they also suggest a particular line the examiner wants you to discuss.
  iii) Direct or straightforward questions, often beginning with the word 'what' or 'why'. Wich such questions it is normally a relatively simple matter to identify the aspects of the topic on which you should concentrate, but as the examiner offers no particular view for you to support or disagree with, the danger is that you will fall into the trap of writing a largely narrative essay.

The four essays above include examples of all three types. Match the essay titles to the essay type.

b) Having identified the subject of the essay, list the issues or topics you would need to include in your answer.

c) Three of the questions require a discussion of an assertion. In each case, list all the main points in *favour* of the assertion, and then list the points *against*.

d) Decide the order in which to make your points.

e) Write your essay.

If you feel comfortable with these questions, you can feel confident about coping with any question on this topic that you might face in the examination.

Further Reading

Most general histories of eighteenth-century Europe contain chapters summarising the ideas and influence of the enlightened writers. Amongst the most accessible are the relevant chapters in:

M. S. Anderson, *Europe in the Eighteen Century* (Longman, 1976)
L. Krieger, *Kings and Philosophers* (Norton, 1970)
S. Andrews, *Eighteenth Century Europe* (Longman, 1965)

There is also the old Historical Association pamphlet:

F. Hartung, *Enlightened Despotism* (1957)

which argues strongly in favour both for the existence of Enlightened Despotism, and that it had positive effects on Europe. It is biased and misleading in places, but provides vigorous defence of the theory.

Of the major rulers, Joseph II has been largely ignored by British historians. Students may find the two-volume biography by **T. Beales** too detailed to cope with and should stick to the elderly but well-written:

S. Padover, *The Revolutionary Emperor* (Eyre & Spottiswoode, 1967)

This should be followed by an excellent short study with documents:

T. C. W. Blanning, *Joseph II and Enlightened Despotism* (Longman, 1970)

Both Frederick II and Catherine II have been the subject of many biographies, and preference is largely a matter of personal taste. On Frederick:

A. Palmer, *Frederick the Great* (Weidenfeld & Nicolson, 1974)

is brief and lively, and includes an interesting discussion of his impact on the later history of Germany. Another useful biography is:

L. Reiners, *Frederick the Great* (New English Library, 1975)

Biographers of Catherine II either tend to write dry academic works, or concentrate on her scandalous love-life. A recent work that tries to give a balanced picture is:

J. Alexander, *Catherine the Great: Life and Legend* (OUP, 1989)

Any biography of Catherine should be backed up with the detailed analysis of:

I. de Madariaga, *Russia in the Age of Catherine the Great* (Weidenfeld & Nicolson, 1981)

which gives a cool and well-researched assessment of her impact on Russian society. If you do not have time to read the whole book, the Epilogue and Conclusions give an excellent summary of her reign and importance.

Sources on Enlightened Despotism

Relatively little has been published in English on the Enlightened Despots. The most useful source books are:

S. Andrews, *Enlightened Despotism* (Longman, 1968)

This is divided into two parts. In Part 1 there are extracts from historians on different aspects of Enlightened Despotism. More accessible are the collection of documents in Part 2. In the same series is

J. Lively, *The Enlightenment* (Longman, 1966)

which gives extracts from some of the works of the *philosophes* and historians' comments on them. The sources chosen are often quite difficult ones.

There is no substitute for sampling the work of the *philosophes* at first hand. Of the works mentioned in the text, two are short and readily available in Penguin editions:

Voltaire, *Candide*

is lively and as racy and unlikely as a modern soap.

J. J. Rousseau, *The Social Contract*

is brief and worth a read, although some of its concepts are not easy to understand.

Other books which include useful sources are:

S. Andrews, *Eighteenth Century Europe* (Longman, 1965)
T. C. W. Blanning, *Joseph II and Enlightened Despotism* (Longman, 1970)

Acknowledgements

The publishers would like to thank the following for permission to use copyright illustrations:

Michael Holford (cover); Bulloz (page 17); The Mansell Collection (pages 37 and 89); Edimedia (Snark International) (page 67); The Trustees of the British Museum (page 80).

Index